"In this insightful book, Velarde ~~provides a great~~ ____ ____ ____ ~~ian~~ families who love movies. His analysis of Pixar movies in light of their themes of identity, friendship, family, courage, ambition and other values is a great help for those who want a fuller, richer experience from their movie viewing. He helps to draw out important values from Pixar movies that illuminate for the viewer/reader that these movies are much more than family-friendly entertainment; they are modern parables of wisdom and virtue."

Brian Godawa, screenwriter, *To End All Wars,* and author, *Hollywood Worldviews: Watching Films with Wisdom and Discernment*

"Robert Velarde has made an interesting and thoughtful contribution to film and philosophy literature. He avoids an overly simplistic analysis without getting bogged down in heavy moral philosophy. Not only will this book help readers gain a deeper understanding of virtue ethics, it will increase their appreciation of one of the best studios in film history."

Douglas M. Beaumont, author, *The Message Behind the Movie*

"Robert Velarde's fascinating book *The Wisdom of Pixar* reminds us why Jesus engaged the culture of his time through the power of stories. After reading the book I wonder if the next generation of teaching pastors may be filmmakers. Velarde has done a great service by reminding us that virtue indeed matters, perhaps now more than ever."

Phil Cooke, CEO, Cooke Pictures, and author, *Branding Faith*

"Wow. And here I thought I was just watching cartoons with my kids! I love how Robert takes readers through the beauty, fun, depth and warmth of Pixar films and frames the solid values that run through them. This book is a must-read for parents who love Pixar films as much as their kids—and for those interested in generating some great postfilm family conversations."

Caryn Rivadeneira, author, *Mama's Got a Fake I.D.,* and cofounder, TheMommyRevolution.com

The WISDOM of PIXAR

An Animated Look at Virtue

Robert Velarde

AN UNAUTHORIZED & UNOFFICIAL GUIDE

IVP Books

An imprint of InterVarsity Press
Downers Grove, Illinois

InterVarsity Press
P.O. Box 1400, Downers Grove, IL 60515-1426
World Wide Web: www.ivpress.com
E-mail: email@ivpress.com

InterVarsity Press® is the book-publishing division of InterVarsity Christian Fellowship/USA®, a movement of students and faculty active on campus at hundreds of universities, colleges and schools of nursing in the United States of America, and a member movement of the International Fellowship of Evangelical Students. For information about local and regional activities, write Public Relations Dept., InterVarsity Christian Fellowship/USA, 6400 Schroeder Rd., P.O. Box 7895, Madison, WI 53707-7895, or visit the IVCF website at <www.intervarsity.org>.

Scripture quotations, unless otherwise noted, are from The Holy Bible, English Standard Version, copyright © 2001 by Crossway Bibles, a division of Good News Publishers. Used by permission. All rights reserved.

Design: Cindy Kiple

Images: party balloons: james steidl/iStockphoto
blue water splash: Irina Tischenko/iStockphoto
clownfish: Gennadij Kurilin/iStockphoto

ISBN 978-0-8308-3297-2

Printed in the United States of America ∞

 InterVarsity Press is committed to protecting the environment and to the responsible use of natural resources. As a member of Green Press Initiative we use recycled paper whenever possible. To learn more about the Green Press Initiative, visit <www.greenpressinitiative.org>.

Library of Congress Cataloging-in-Publication Data

Velarde, Robert, 1969-
 The wisdom of Pixar: an animated look at virtue / Robert Velarde.
  p. cm.
 Includes bibliographical references and index.
 ISBN 978-0-8308-3297-2 (pbk.: alk. paper)
 1. Animated films—History and criticism. 2. Motion
pictures—Religious aspects—Christianity. 3. Pixar (Firm) I. Title.
 PN1997.5.V47 2010
 791.43'34—dc22

                                                          2010008334

P	18	17	16	15	14	13	12	11	10	9	8	7	6	5	4	3	2	1
Y	25	24	23	22	21	20	19	18	17	16	15	14	13	12	11	10		

For Marcus,
a great fan of *Cars*
(especially "Mr. The King")

CONTENTS

INTRODUCTION

Toy Story. *Finding Nemo. Ratatouille. WALL-E. Up.* All of these endearing films come from a common source: Pixar Animation Studios. From its formation as an independent company in 1986 through its purchase by Disney in 2006 for a sum of $7.4 billion, Pixar has enjoyed an unbroken string of box office success. Families the world over have come to trust the Pixar brand and its breathtaking computer-generated depictions of toys, fish, rats, robots, cars and more.

But Pixar films aren't just for children. Pixar movies and their themes resonate with kids and adults alike because of the attention-grabbing animation, but that is not the sole factor. The stories told in Pixar films are also a key element of their appeal, as are the characters. Even though we may be watching toys or cars that are brought to life, or monsters or even rats, these characters contain a quality of reality to which we can relate. Moreover, in our often dark and negative world, Pixar films offer hope, imagination, beauty and a degree of purity and innocence that is countercultural in our age.

Yes, human nature has a dark side. It is capably depicted—in much detail—by many gritty, non-Pixar films. Pixar, however, calls our attention back to the almost forgotten world of virtue. We sympathize and perhaps even empathize with the characters in Pixar films because we relate to their struggles. The characters help us understand how to better build our *own* characters—morally speaking, that is. But Pixar doesn't preach to us. There is no First Church of Pixar to offer us sermons, pews, committees, incense or flowing choir robes (though one might say that Pixar does pass around the collection plate before every screening!). Instead, we come to better understand virtue through entertaining and engaging stories.

Pixar tells stories. These stories, in turn, have the power to wholly engage us—heart, soul and mind. The characters and plots need not be overtly Christian in order to instruct us in virtue. Christ engaged his listeners by telling parables, not by preaching to them or delivering dry lectures. He shared stories that have, at their center, practical moral lessons that stick with us. We remember the tales of the good Samaritan and the prodigal son not because they sound like they come from a textbook on ethics, but because they are stories that resonate with us as human beings and capture our interest.

This book does not seek to turn Pixar films into Christian parables, or even to suggest that Pixar's films are somehow secretly Christian. *The Wisdom of Pixar* explores the content of Pixar's films primarily as they relate to virtue and applies the insights practically to the Christian life. The first two chapters provide an overview of the concepts of virtue and wisdom, while also addressing two overarching themes in Pixar films—hope and imagination—and how these themes are relevant to the Christian life. The remaining chapters jump right into the content of Pixar's films by looking at key themes such as identity, justice, friendship, humor, family and several more. Although each chapter highlights a particular Pixar film, each also mentions other Pixar films. At the end of these chapters you'll also find discussion questions suitable for individuals or groups.

If you need a refresher as to the content of the films discussed, see appendix A, "Pixar's Plots." If you haven't seen a particular film addressed in *The Wisdom of Pixar*, it would be best for you to see it first. (That's not a requirement, but it will be more fun if you do!) Finally, appendix B, "Pixar's Short Films," serves, as the title suggests, as a brief guide to some of Pixar's many entertaining short films, while appendix C offers a movie discussion guide suitable for individuals or groups.

Pixar has created a body of work that is entertaining, engaging, endearing and edifying. Let's begin our journey through Pixar's films by exploring virtue and wisdom.

1

VIRTUE & WISDOM

An Animated Look

The conference center is crowded with attendees eager to learn more about the intricacies of moral philosophy. Entering the main lecture hall, you are fortunate to get a seat close enough to see the panel members seated behind a long table. A dignified expression on his face, the panel moderator approaches the lectern while carefully adjusting his hat. As he taps on the microphone you hear him say, "Hello? Check. Is that better? Can everybody hear me? Today's opening panel discussion is about moral philosophy in Pixar films." You listen, confused. You had anticipated an academic gathering of scholars presenting erudite papers on the finer points of ethics. But the speaker is a cowboy doll you recognize from the *Toy Story* films—Woody. You even catch a glimpse of the pull string attached to his back.

"Let me introduce our participants," Woody continues, gesturing to the individuals seated behind the table. "First we have Buzz Lightyear, Space Ranger. To his left is Mr. Potato Head. Next to him we have Hamm and Luxo Jr. Lastly, we have John Lasseter, chief creative officer of Pixar Animation Studios."

Something is not right. You glance at the stage and see a number of characters from the *Toy Story* films. Some are organizing papers and making notes, and others are chatting quietly. You see Buzz Lightyear, a space toy and star of the *Toy Story* films, speaking animatedly to Mr. Potato Head, who is wearing a beret, glasses and a goatee for the occasion. Hamm, the piggy bank, looks bored as he flips a quarter in the air, while the little white Luxo lamp is bobbing its "head," turning its light on and off and bouncing in place. The only human on the stage is John Lasseter, wearing a trademark Hawaiian shirt but looking unusually serious.

A boxy-looking robot passes by and hands you a program. He accidentally drops the remaining pile of programs, then scrambles to collect them all and rushes off. You see a small white robot, looking a tad upset, cleaning up after the boxy robot. This must be some sort of joke. Flipping through your program, you are surprised at the various topics and speakers scheduled: "Aretaic Ethics in the Twenty-First Century," presented by Bo Peep; "The Epistemological Virtues of Animal Rights," an address by Slinky Dog; "A Lasseterian Theory of Moral Philosophy," a preliminary treatise by John Lasseter; and "Emperor Zurg and the Problem of Evil," a peer-reviewed paper by Dr. Buzz Lightyear.

"Today's panel discussion," continues Woody, "will feature an animated look at virtue and wisdom. Following the discussion, questions from attendees are welcome." Woody steps away from the lectern, which you now notice is a blue and red Tinkertoy container. Curious, you settle in for what you hope will be an enlightening discussion of moral philosophy.

I do not intend for you to take this unlikely gathering seriously. Pixar Animation Studios is not working closely with moral philosophers to inject ethical ideologies into its films. Nor is the studio actively engaged in studying arcane aspects of morality, virtue and wisdom in order to infuse films with deep ideas about right and wrong and the meaning of life. Nevertheless, films do tell stories, and in the process of telling stories, they present ideas. As Western culture continues to shift from a "Have you read . . . ?" perspective to a "Have you seen . . . ?" framework, the influence of films increases exponentially.

So while Pixar films do not provide textbook examples of the many facets of moral philosophy, we can still learn much about virtue and wisdom from them. The purpose of this chapter, moreover, is not to attempt a detailed study of ethics, but to provide a sweeping introduction to the topic with a particular emphasis on virtue and wisdom.

The Ethics of Virtue

There are a number of approaches to ethics, each with fine-sounding academic terminology: deontology, metaethics, teleology, divine command theory, utilitarianism, ethical egoism, normative ethics, applied ethics and more. Our goal here, however, is not to delve deeply into these topics. Instead, following a brief definition of ethics, we will look specifically at virtue and wisdom.

Ethics, in short, is a branch of *philosophy*, which means the "love of wisdom." Concerned with right and wrong, ethics is about what ought or ought not to be done. Practically speaking, ethics is about how one should or should not live. The approach taken in this book is primarily that of *virtue ethics* or *virtue theory*, although I certainly incorporate other aspects of ethics, including a distinctly Christian perspective. With roots in Aristotle, Augustine, Aquinas and other thinkers, including Christ, virtue theory places an emphasis on moral character. Building moral character is, consequently, important within this framework. The New Testament is not an ethical philosophy textbook, but it nevertheless does include elements of virtue theory. It encourages, for example, the development of virtues that will help the Christian be more Christlike. Note, too, that virtue theory is sometimes referred to as an *ethic of being*, since its focus is on the character of an individual and his or her ethical development as opposed to clear-cut delineations between right and wrong actions. Virtue-based ethical systems stress the importance of ethical character over rule-based systems. How one lives one's life is the focus of virtue ethics, and character is central to virtue.

Developing moral character and virtue is important, but the system is not without flaws. At some point, virtue theorists must make some appeal to a standard as to what sort of character should be emulated, cultivated and sought after. This is where Christian ethics can step in and provide a solid foundation not only for virtue ethics but for other ethical approaches.

Virtue, Habit and Action

Unfortunately, the concept of virtue in contemporary times is often misunderstood. There's a tendency to connect it to chastity or some sort of puritanical thinking. It's not incorrect to use virtue in these senses, but the concept encompasses much more. It touches on, for example, morality, right and wrong, good and evil, concepts related to justice, courage, love and more. For ancient philosophers, virtue was important in relation to defining the good life, as well as what makes a person or a society good. As such, virtue for the ancients was related to happiness or what is called *eudaemonism*—viewing happiness and morality as being intertwined in the pursuit of the good life. The term *happiness*, too, may cause confusion here. Today we primarily think of happiness in a limited scope, as a particular state of mind that brings us joy, pleasure and contentment. But to Aristotle, the term encompassed our moral well-being and, in short, living life well. Prudence, or what may be called *practical wisdom*, is also tied to virtue. But we'll get to the topic of wisdom later.

Plato and Aristotle, though they certainly had their share of disagreements, both linked virtue to prudence (wisdom), justice, temperance and courage—the four so-called cardinal virtues. They also viewed virtue as being both an inner and an outer quality. Virtue is internal, in that it is the character within us that struggles with ethical choices intellectually. It is also external, in that virtue must express itself outwardly through the actions and behavior that result from our choices. Being virtuous, then, is about more than just reading or studying or knowing—it's about living virtue and building character. For the Christian, the natural or cardinal virtues are not enough. We also need distinctly Christian virtues rooted in God such as faith, hope and love (the so-called theological virtues).

Another element of virtue ethics has to do with habit. Here thinkers like Aquinas, though not exclusively so, focus on character-building through habit. More recently, Christian thinker C. S. Lewis also emphasized virtue ethics and habit in books such as *Mere Christianity*. The concept of habit helping to build character and virtue is not without criticism, however. Can virtue be taught like mathematics? Is virtue just a habit, so that all we need do is practice it in order for it to "work," in a pragmatic sense? Or does virtue have a transcendent source? A typical Christian response would likely claim that virtue, being moral goodness, is rooted in God's supreme goodness and, as such, cannot be taught; at the same time, it might say that we can learn to bring out God-given virtues in our lives. Some thinkers, such as Augustine, have argued that the ultimate Christian foundation for ethics is God's love. We will return to this topic in chapter twelve.

The ethical counterpart to virtue is vice. In Plato's *Republic*, he says, "So virtue, as it seems, is a kind of health and excellence and good state of the soul, but vice is disease and deformity and weakness."[1] In short, if virtue is right and thus desirable, then vice is wrong and thus undesirable.

Virtue is not limited to the individual, though that is of course the place where it must begin. If we are to influence the world for the glory of God, we must first be influenced ourselves. But virtue needs action. Social justice—actively making a difference in a suffering world—is an example of virtue in action: not out of pride or some other misguided purpose, but because God's love compels us to make a difference. Virtue, in this sense, may be its own reward, as Marcus Aurelius stated. In Christian terms, everything we do that is truly virtuous comes to us by God's love and grace rather than from our own fallen and depraved nature. Wisdom and virtue should move us to practical action, not just to sitting around and thinking about how wise and virtuous we may or may not be.

The Prime Wisdom

Virtue and wisdom are connected. Wisdom is, in fact, a virtue. It is a valued character trait and returns us to the issue of living life morally well. How do we know the right way to live? Wisdom helps us. The ability to make sound judgments is also associated with wisdom. To be wise, after all, is to demonstrate good judgment as applied to life. Although we make progress over the centuries in technological and other advancements, the same cannot generally be said of wisdom. Each age—and, in turn, each individual—must cultivate wisdom. In other words, historically wisdom has not been shown to grow and advance as humans have done in other areas. Individuals become wiser, but the same does not apply to humanity as a whole. Have we lost interest in wisdom and replaced it with interest in progress or technology (see chapter eleven)?

Plato emphasized justice in his *Republic*, but in his *Laws*, it is the virtue of wisdom that is paramount. Aristotle, too, in his *Politics*, linked virtue and wisdom. Augustine even developed a seven-step plan for wisdom, though it is certainly not of the self-help, pop psychology variety. Aquinas saw wisdom as did the Bible— that is, as being established in "the fear of the LORD" (Psalm 111:10;

Proverbs 9:10). Wisdom is not the exclusive domain of Christians, either. Both Augustine and Aquinas viewed non-Christian wisdom as foreshadowing distinctly Christian wisdom. As such, Aquinas viewed the natural wisdom of Aristotle as valuable. Likewise, we should not shy away from wisdom simply because it is found in something such as a computer-animated film.

In *Paradise Lost*, Milton wrote, "That which before us lies in daily life, Is the prime Wisdom."[2] In a very real sense, the "prime Wisdom" in Christianity is God. From him flows wisdom, perfect moral virtue and holiness. Both testaments have much to say about wisdom. In the Old Testament, wisdom is personified as a divine attribute through the use of poetic language (see Proverbs 8, for instance). There is even a recognized biblical genre known as *Wisdom literature* that includes Job, Proverbs and Ecclesiastes. Distinctly divine wisdom is mentioned in numerous passages, including 1 Kings 3:28, Ezra 7:25, Job 12:13 and Luke 11:49. The common New Testament word for wisdom is *sophia*, used in the word *philosophy*, which, again, means the "love of wisdom."

There is also a sense in which human wisdom alone is not really the sort of wisdom God desires. In 1 Corinthians 1:20, for instance, we read, "Where is the one who is wise? Where is the scribe? Where is the debater of this age? Has not God made foolish the wisdom of the world?" There are a few ways we can make sense of such a passage. We can view the passage as emphasizing the greatness and supreme goodness and wisdom of God as being far beyond anything we as humans may consider wise. It may also be viewed as demonstrating the inadequacies of human wisdom alone; that is, the limitations of human wisdom apart from God. There's also a worldview aspect to the passage, insofar as any worldview that does not have its foundation in God and his revealed truths is inadequate to explain reality and provide a solution to the human dilemma. The wisdom that Paul is imparting, guided by the Holy Spirit, is in fact divine wisdom, not ordinary wisdom. In other words, the wisdom of God is by definition extraordinary and, as such, we would do well to heed it.

What is it that enriches life? Biblically speaking, it is a virtuous life rooted in God. As Proverbs 3:13-14 puts it, "Blessed is the one who finds wisdom, and the one who gets understanding, for the gain from her [wisdom personified] is better than gain from silver and her profit better than gold." A life worth living is founded in virtue and wisdom, which are in turn established in God. In the New Testament it is Christ, being in the perfect image of God, who is our example of the perfect wisdom of God (1 Corinthians 1:24). It is Christ "in whom are hidden all the treasures of wisdom and knowledge" (Colossians 2:3).

Practical Ethics

It's important to reiterate the fact that reading and learning about ethics should not remain an armchair hobby. Ethics carries a practical relevance, as other chapters in this book seek to emphasize in relation to Pixar films. Ethical matters are a regular occurrence in everyday life. Sometimes the moral choices we face concern fairly simple matters, while other times ethical challenges are difficult and of great significance. Over time it is in our best interest to seek to cultivate virtue in our lives and, by doing so, to cultivate character.

As a virtue, wisdom is foundational; so also is love. Indeed, God's love is what should move each of us to pursue godly virtue. What aspects of virtue and wisdom can Pixar films impart to us? Later chapters emphasize ten aspects, selected not necessarily because they are the central themes of the films with which they are associated but because of their significance. But before we get there, let's take some time to address two recurring and overarching themes that Pixar films communicate: hope and imagination.

Discussion Questions

1. Virtue-oriented ethics emphasize building character. How can habit play a role in this process?

2. What do you think about gaining insights into wisdom and virtue from non-Christian sources?

3. Have film and television displaced books as the predominant form of entertainment? Why or why not? In either case, to what extent do films influence individuals and culture?

4. According to the New Testament example of the wisdom of God, Christians should seek to imitate Christ. What virtues did he demonstrate? What wisdom did he offer?

5. List at least two specific examples that Christ left us regarding virtues we can emulate. If you have difficulty thinking of examples, read the parable of the good Samaritan and discuss elements of virtue you find in the story (see Luke 10:25-37).

2

HOPE & IMAGINATION

"To infinity and beyond!"

In *Finding Nemo*, after they have escaped from a hungry shark and massive minefield explosions, the fish Marlin and Dory are exhausted. Marlin is anxious to find his missing son, Nemo, but now he has lost his best clue for finding him—a scuba mask inscribed with the address of the diver who captured Nemo. Discouraged, Marlin doesn't know what to do. "That was my only chance at finding my son; now it's gone!" But Dory is not so easily deterred. "Hey, Mr. Grumpy Gills," she begins, "When life gets you down, you know what you gotta do? Just keep swimming, just keep swimming, just keep swimming, swimming, swimming. What do we do? We swim, swim." Dory continues joyfully singing about swimming, while leading Marlin into the dark ocean depths in search of the mask. Despair has engulfed Marlin, while Dory remains hopeful in the face of adversity. Pixar films have a way of bringing out the hopeful side of life, moving us to "just keep swimming" no matter what our circumstances.

But there's more to Pixar films than an overarching theme of hope; they are also full of imagination. In Pixar's first feature film, *Toy Story*, toys come alive when humans aren't around. Woody the cowboy doll climbs onto a bed and sees an imposing action figure. It's a Space Ranger, otherwise known as Buzz Lightyear. Buzz, who doesn't know he's a toy, attempts to contact Star Command and is puzzled by their silence. Distraught over the damage to his "ship"—the cardboard box he came in—Buzz makes a voice recording in his mission log, noting that he has crash landed on a "strange planet." Woody greets Buzz, as do the other toys in the room. When Woody refers to Buzz as a toy, the Space Ranger is not amused, resulting in some banter as to whether or not Buzz can really fly. Buzz sets out to demonstrate his flying prowess and as he prepares to jump from a bedpost, he utters the now-famous phrase, "To infinity and beyond!" Lightyear's words may very well be a call to creativity and imagination too. That's certainly been the case for Pixar, as the studio continues to dream up fantastic adventures that are also grounded in realities to which many can relate.

This chapter will focus on two important themes that Pixar films explore: hope and imagination. Hope and imagination are relevant not only to the movies but also to everyday life, as well as to specific applications within the Christian life. Let's begin by taking a look at hope in general, hope as depicted in Pixar films and a biblical view of hope.

Pixar's Hope

Trends in filmmaking come and go, but there's always room for hopeful films, such as the classic *It's a Wonderful Life*. Some films, however, emphasize the darkness of our world—the ugly reality of a world ripped apart by sin (*The Dark Knight* is a good contemporary example of this kind). While it's important to understand the depravity manifested in the world, it's also important to affirm the joys, opportunities and hopes open to us. In this respect, Pixar films excel to the point that some might consider the films countercultural in their positive affirmations. This does not mean that Pixar avoids challenging topics; rather, the studio handles them in such a way as to leave hope intact.

Pixar's film *WALL-E*, for instance, is about a polluted earth. Human-produced garbage is everywhere, even in space, where thousands of discarded satellites orbit the planet. After trashing the planet and departing to space, humans leave the messy job of cleaning it up to robots like WALL-E, the main character, a Waste Allocation Load Lifter—Earth Class. Nevertheless, the opening song from *Hello, Dolly!*—"Put on Your Sunday Clothes"—immediately sets an optimistic, hopeful tone, while computer-generated images of the wonders of space dazzle viewers. Despite playing over images of a trashed and abused earth, the hopeful, upbeat song praises the wonder and joy in the world. Skyscraper-sized piles of garbage are not enough to dampen the spirits of *WALL-E*, a film that is, in the end, primarily about love (with a good dose of philosophy of technology too).

Up, true to its name, is also uplifting. While it includes its share of the realities of human suffering, in the end *Up* is a hopeful film. Through a fantastic adventure, grumpy old man Carl Fredricksen learns to enjoy life again, befriends a boy in need and realizes that even though the love of his life, Ellie, is gone, she'd want him to enjoy the adventure that still awaits.

Faith, Hope and Love

Along with faith and love, hope is one of three important Christian virtues (1 Corinthians 13:13; Colossians 1:5; 1 Thessalonians 1:3; 5:8). Hope by its very nature is opposed to hopelessness (despair). The Bible refers to "the God of hope," linking "joy and peace" to hope that is founded on belief in God (Romans 15:13). Christian hope requires faith in God and his goodness. His love or, we might say, his *omnibenevolence*, is foundational to hope.

While the Old Testament emphasis is on hope in God the Father, the New Testament emphasizes faith in God the Son. Paul refers to Jesus as "Christ Jesus our hope" (1 Timothy 1:1). The primary example of the hope Christ offers is the reality of his resurrection from the dead. This, in turn, gives us hope in the future healing and restoration of creation that God has promised, as well as the complete manifestation of his kingdom—the *eschaton*, or the climactic end of God-directed history.

While hope in general is about having a positive attitude about the future, the biblical dimension adds God as the focal point of hope. Consequently, hope is not a technique; it is not to be placed on a particular field of inquiry such as science and technology, or in politics or individuals no matter how influential they may be. Christian hope, rather, is God-directed. In short, if God exists, there is hope. The Christian view of hope should move us to engage our world positively in areas such as social justice—not because we can perfect the world on our own, but because we know there is a purposeful direction to history that is guided by God and because we are to emulate Christ's compassion in helping others.

It's easy to become discouraged by the spirit of our age. While things often seem hopeless, the Christian virtue of hope calls us to focus on God. It is the task of the Christian to offer hope grounded in the reality provided by the living God. With hope comes an opportunity to leave behind despair in exchange for the meaning found in the Christian worldview. Here, imagination can help us along as we grapple with the challenges of life and the culture that surrounds us.

Pixar's Imagination

Imagination is part of human nature. The creative spark is hardwired into us. Imagination drives times of leisure, artistic creativity and escape into fantastic realms, whether these pursuits occur through literature, music, painting, film or other human expres-

sions. Every Pixar film is creative and imaginative. But where do
creativity and imagination come from? What is their role in daily
life? Are some forms of imagination harmful? Does creativity
originate in being made in God's image? Having some understanding of the nature and role of imagination will help us better understand the role of virtue in imagination and how it, too, can help us
become better people.

It's clear that Pixar values creativity and imagination. Along
with placing emphasis on telling a good story, Pixar films thrive
on creative and imaginative characters and settings. They do not
overlook the unique and varied expressions of artistic creativity in
humans. A film about a rat who wants to be a chef, *Ratatouille* is
clear regarding its admiration for the human imagination. As the
main character, Remy, explains it, "I know I'm supposed to hate
humans, but there's something about them. They don't just survive, they discover, they create!" The human character Chef Gusteau underscores human creativity when he compares the making
of a gourmet meal to the artistry of music: "Good food is like music you can taste, color you can smell. There is excellence all
around you. You need only be aware to stop and savor it."

Imagination is also valued in *Toy Story* and *Toy Story 2*. Both
films feature scenes of the boy Andy playing with his toys. His
play naturally involves imagination. *Toy Story* begins with an old
West bank robbery, spearheaded by Mr. Potato Head no less (aka
"One-Eyed Bart"). It takes the cowboy doll Woody to save the day
(and also his dinosaur, Rex, who happens to eat force-field dogs).
In *Toy Story 2*, Andy is undeterred by the fact that he's supposed
to leave for cowboy camp with his mom and sister in just five minutes. Instead, those minutes turn into an opportunity for creativity and imagination. This time Bo Peep is being held captive by
evil Dr. Pork Chop, complete with black bowler hat and an army
of toy soldiers at his disposal. In order to save Bo Peep from being
eaten by a shark or the ever-popular "death by monkeys," Andy

brings in Buzz Lightyear to join forces with Woody; together they save the day.

The extent of creativity expressed by human beings, whether children or adults, is completely unique to humans. We tell stories, play with toys, create visual artwork, compose music and write books; in short, we imagine and bring to life ideas rich in creativity. We delight in being clever and in being entertained by human creativity.

Creativity in God's Image

Where does imagination originate? Biblically speaking, it derives from the fact that human beings alone are said to be made in God's image (Genesis 1:26-27). The so-called *imago Dei* is what drives us creatively, imaginatively, intellectually, morally, spiritually and more. As Cheryl Forbes has astutely observed, "Imagination is the image of God in us."[1] Or, as Christian thinker Francis Schaeffer put it, "The Christian is the one whose imagination should fly beyond the stars."[2] Why? Because the Christian worldview offers us a firm foundation for human creativity and imagination. As God is creative, so to a lesser extent are we. The Bible itself is rich in imagery, vivid word pictures and captivating storytelling. The extent of creativity in human beings may even be used as one line of argumentation for the existence of God. In a world that is supposedly the result of blind chance and time, why should we consider anything to be beautiful or creative or imaginative in any sense? Relevant to our purposes in later chapters is the idea that the image of God in us grants us the capacity to live as moral beings.

Not everything we create and imagine is perfectly holy, of course. Like anything good, imagination can be warped by human depravity. At times we may overindulge in imagination and fantasy rather than concentrating on the real world, or in some instances imagination becomes destructive. As John Weldon and James Bjornstad have stated:

Fantasy is actually a part of God's creation in the sense that God created man with imagination and the ability to fantasize. . . . But fantasy is not justified in itself. Just because fantasy in general is part of God's creation, no specific fantasy is necessarily right or good. . . . Even "good" fantasy can be corrupted by overindulgence. . . . There is also a distorted and destructive use (e.g., the fantasizing of sexual exploits or extreme violence toward someone).[3]

Yet while fantasy and imagination can open the door to danger, that does not rule out the possibility of communicating Christian truth via imagination. Many things can potentially lead to sin, but the wise and discerning Christian can take such things, like imagination, and use them for God's glory. In his first letter to the Corinthian believers, Paul writes: "'Everything is permissible for me'—but not everything is beneficial. 'Everything is permissible for me'—but I will not be mastered by anything" (1 Corinthians 6:12 NIV).

W. Harold Mare comments, "Every action we contemplate should be tested by two questions: 'Is it beneficial' and 'Will it overpower and enslave me and so have a detrimental effect on the church and my testimony for Christ?'"[4] Commenting on Matthew 5:29-30, where Jesus figuratively suggests extreme measures be taken "if your right eye causes you to sin" or "if your right hand causes you to sin," D. A. Carson writes, "Imagination is a God-given gift; but if it is fed dirt by the eye, it will be dirty. All sin . . . begins with the imagination. Therefore what feeds the imagination is of maximum importance in the pursuit of kingdom righteousness."[5] There are potential woes of imagination, but that does not mean that imagination pursued in a wholesome manner must be discarded.

The Moral of the Story
Our hope is placed in God, supported by his love and grasped by our faith. Hope is pointless unless something behind it ensures

that our positive outlook is grounded in a reality we can trust. Moreover, imagination is indeed God's image at work in and through us. He has bestowed us with incredible amounts of creativity. Properly directed, our imagination can contribute positively toward making a difference in the world. Also, because we are made in God's image, we are by nature moral beings. Whether we are Christian or not, we sense the pull of God's natural law in our lives on a daily basis. Learning more about these virtues will help us grow in character. Stories offer us numerous examples of vice and virtue, and we hope that the latter will grow in us while the former will diminish.

While hope and imagination are overarching themes that run consistently through Pixar films, each film also touches on key virtues, offering wise insights along the way. In the remaining chapters we'll look at ten examples of the wisdom of Pixar, beginning with the topic of identity in *Toy Story*.

Discussion Questions

1. How is hope relevant to virtue?

2. What are some differences between hope in general and hope of a distinctly Christian character?

3. How does human imagination serve as an argument for the existence of God?

4. Discuss hope and imagination as expressed in one or more Pixar films. How do the topics play out in the films you have selected? What other films can you think of that offer hope?

IDENTITY

Toy Story—
"You are a toy!"

Strange things are happening to Woody the cowboy doll. He used to be Andy's favorite toy, but not anymore. Ever since the sudden birthday party appearance of the space toy Buzz Lightyear, Woody feels out of place and somewhat jealous. Woody, however, isn't the only one with problems. Waking up one morning in a toy box, rather than his usual spot on Andy's bed, Woody has had enough of Buzz. "All right," says an exasperated Woody, "That's it!" He stomps over to Buzz, who is busily working on repairing his spaceship (the cardboard box he came in). After warning Buzz to stay away from Andy, Woody adds, "Stop with this space man thing. It's getting on my nerves!" When Woody pushes Buzz and the space toy's helmet opens, Buzz falls to the floor, gasping for air, surprised that the air isn't toxic. "You actually think," says Woody, "you're *the* Buzz Lightyear?" But it will take more than this encounter for Buzz to accept his true identity.

The concept of identity is significant. Who we are shapes what we do, but what we do also shapes who we are. If we lack a healthy understanding of the concept of identity, we will wander through life uncertain about what to do with ourselves. As in the case of Buzz Lightyear, the lack of understanding of one's identity can actually be a form of deception. Knowing the truth about who we are and what we were made for is important. What, in general, is identity? What, specifically, is a Christian concept of identity? Does identity relate to wisdom and virtue? How can computer-generated films help us with the concept of identity? These are the questions that we will seek to answer.

ACTION!

Toy Story
U.S. Release Date: November 22, 1995

The road to fame for the world's first computer-animated feature film, *Toy Story,* was far from a given. While the basic storyline remained the same from its inception—toys that want children to play with them—many other factors developed and changed along the way. The lead role, for instance, was originally envisioned as Tinny from the Pixar short film *Tin Toy* (see appendix B), while an early version of Buzz Lightyear was named Lunar Larry. The screenplay, too, went through many iterations, ultimately crediting four people, including Joss Whedon, who would later go on to success with *Buffy the Vampire Slayer.*

Who Am I?

Identity is both simple and complex. On a rudimentary level, identity has to do with who we are. As such, it addresses a fundamental philosophical question: "Who am I?" Identity is also complex and multifaceted. Numerous influences contribute to shaping our identity, including our family background, ethnicity, cultural environment, vocational inclinations, religious adherence, moral choices and more. If we are unable to establish a healthy identity, confusion and unhappiness usually result.

While one can approach the question of identity in a variety of ways, the Christian position on the matter is unique. Identity for

the Christian is first and foremost found in God. This is the case
because we are made in God's image (Genesis 1:26-27), a concept
broached in chapter two in relation to human creativity. The image of God in us is key to understanding our identity and purpose,
as well as to restoring our relationship with God. In the New Testament, Christ is representative of the image of God (2 Corinthians 4:4; Colossians 1:15), thus providing us with an example of
what God's image looks like. Although much more could be said
on the topic, its relevance here is on identity in relation to virtue.
The image of God encompasses the moral realm, which is why we
are moral creatures. If our worldview has a proper foundation in
God, then so should our identity. Consequently, our moral choices
will reflect this fact.

Identity is relevant to the Christian both in an individual sense
and in relation to the church as a whole. Individually, our identity
in Christ relates to the concept of calling. What is the Christian
calling? In a general sense, *calling* refers to God's work in relation
to restoring the broken relationship with human beings. Special
calling, on the other hand, has to do with God working specifically in the life of an individual, leading her or him to an opportunity to place faith in Christ. There's also a further concept known
as an effectual call, which is relevant to God's grace and forgive-
ness. For our purposes here, however, general and special calling
are sufficient examples.

As Christians, we are called to serve God both in this world
and in the afterlife. This means, on a practical level, that our calling should move us to make a difference in the world. We need to
share God's truth and demonstrate the love of God by our actions,
an idea which leads us back again to the concept of virtue. It's not
enough to be a Christian and do nothing much about it. God calls
us to positively interact in the world.

Identity also relates to the church as a whole: God's people as
represented throughout the world in various expressions of wor-

ship. If the church is not so different in its behavior than the negative aspects of culture around it, then God's people are having an
identity crisis. But if the church is truly establishing its identity in
God, his calling and his purposes, then we can indeed provide
light in the darkness.

Pixar's Identity

Identity, calling and purpose are critical concepts. It would be
naive, of course, to think that Pixar Animation Studios gathered
together with the specific intent to address deep philosophical
questions of human identity, calling, purpose and the meaning of
life. These are family films intended primarily as entertainment.
Nevertheless, the films do offer us several examples relevant to
identity. When Helen (aka Elastigirl) in *The Incredibles* tells her
daughter, "Your identity is your most valuable possession; protect
it," is it a stretch (pun intended) to apply these words beyond the
immediate context? As a superhero, Helen knows it's important to
keep her true identity secret, and she is imparting this wisdom to
her daughter. But on another level, identity is indeed a valuable
possession, establishing who we are and what our purpose is in
this world. Three Pixar films will serve as examples for us here:
Toy Story, Toy Story 2 and *Ratatouille*.

You Are a Child's Plaything!

We have already established Buzz Lightyear's identity crisis.
Put simply, he doesn't realize that he is a toy. Instead, he thinks
he is a real Space Ranger, charged with protecting and saving
the galaxy. Two additional scenes from *Toy Story* will serve to
demonstrate the concept of identity. The first involves Woody
and Buzz when they are lost at a Dinoco gas station. Woody immediately realizes the seriousness of the situation, crying out,
"I'm a lost toy!" Buzz, however, is still deluded, believing that
he is a Space Ranger on an important mission. When Buzz goes

on about the "security of this entire universe" being in jeopardy because of Woody, the cowboy doll has had enough. Unable to contain himself, Woody yells at Buzz, "You are a toy! You aren't the real Buzz Lightyear . . . you're an action figure! You are a child's plaything!" But Buzz will have none of it and remains convinced he's a Space Ranger. "You are a sad, strange little man," Buzz replies to Woody, "and you have my pity." It will take another more jarring encounter for Buzz to realize the truth about his identity.

After a series of misadventures, Buzz and Woody end up being captured by the malicious boy Sid. During an escape attempt, Woody and Buzz must hide quickly or risk being chewed up by Sid's vicious dog, Scud. Buzz dashes into a room where a television is on and hears a message, "Calling Buzz Lightyear! Come in, Buzz Lightyear. This is Star Command." Momentarily excited, thinking it is a real message for him, Buzz is then faced with a television commercial advertising Buzz Lightyear action figures. Complete with the over-the-top voice of Penn Jillette of "Penn and Teller" notoriety as the narrator, the commercial announces, "The world's greatest superhero, now the world's greatest toy! Buzz has it all!" Buzz watches in confusion as he sees himself on television demonstrating his karate-chop action, pulsating laser light, voice simulator and high-pressure space wings (accompanied on screen by the humiliating words "NOT A FLYING TOY").

Buzz is stunned. As if for the first time he notices the phrase "Made in Taiwan" on the inside cover of a compartment on his arm. Randy Newman's song, "I Will Go Sailing No More," begins to play, underscoring Buzz's realization that he is, in fact, just a toy. But Buzz still can't accept his true identity. Grasping for his identity as a Space Ranger, Buzz decides to attempt to fly. His brave attempt is met with the reality that he can't do it. He's not a Space Ranger at all; he's a toy just like Woody told him he was. Crashing to the floor, Buzz breaks an arm and lies on the floor defeated, helpless and confused. "I'm just a toy—a stupid little insignificant toy," says Buzz.

Fortunately, Buzz isn't left in despair. For a time he gives up hope, but Woody explains to the Space Ranger how important it is to be a toy. Woody encourages Buzz to be what he was made to be: a great toy that can make a child happy.

Woody's Roundup

In *Toy Story 2* the tables are turned. Woody knows he is a toy, but he has lost sight of what that means. His identity crisis has moved him to desire to travel to a toy museum in Japan, where he'll be on display with other toys and memorabilia associated with a fictional classic television series called *Woody's Roundup* (which is reminiscent of the vintage television program *Howdy Doody*).

The shift in Woody's thinking about his identity is not immediate. It begins with concerns about being damaged as a toy, knowing that he won't last forever and that at some point Andy will grow up and not want to play with toys anymore. Incidentally, this fear is somewhat realized in *Toy Story 3* when Andy, getting ready to go to college, loses his toys to a daycare center where toys are routinely treated roughly. Where will Woody be then? Is it worth it to stick with Andy and his fellow toys, or is traveling to Japan to be part of a museum collection a better option? Similarly to how Buzz encountered his true identity through a television commercial in *Toy Story*, Woody is confronted with a situation that sheds light on his identity as well: he sees an excerpt from the television show *Woody's Roundup*. Woody had no idea who he was, as fellow toy Prospector (aka Stinky Pete) points out, "Why, you don't know who you are, do you?" As it turns out, Woody is part of the world of *Woody's Roundup* and is in fact also a valuable collector's item.

Initially reluctant to leave behind his toy friends and the boy Andy, Woody eventually decides to travel to the toy museum and, for a time, is excited and happy about the opportunity. That changes when Buzz, Rex, Mr. Potato Head, Hamm and Slinky Dog unexpectedly come to rescue Woody. Buzz tries to convince Woody to return with him to Andy's house: "Woody, stop this nonsense and let's go . . . you're not a collector's item, you're a child's plaything. You are a toy!" Woody has forgotten what he taught Buzz, namely, that "life's only worth living if you're being loved by a kid." In this case Woody knows he is a toy, so that aspect of identity is not mysterious. Yet Woody is struggling with another aspect of his identity; that is, what is it that he is supposed to do as a toy? Analogously, each of us knows that we are human; but what is it that we are supposed to do with ourselves as humans?

I Need to Rethink My Life

The Pixar film *Ratatouille* also addresses issues regarding identity, though not as overtly as the *Toy Story* films. Remy is a rat who also happens to enjoy cooking. His identity is tied to his ambition to be a chef (see chapter ten), but is obviously hampered by the fact that he's not human. As a rat, Remy is not expected to be interested in gourmet cooking or to associate with humans, yet Remy does both. He befriends the bungling young man Alfredo Linguini, and together they hatch a plan to pass Linguini off as a talented chef (while in reality Remy does all the work). From Remy's opening narration, we learn that he's in the middle of an identity crisis. Jumping out of the window of a home while carrying the book *Anyone Can Cook!* Remy explains via a voice-over, "This is me. I think it's apparent I need to rethink my life a little bit. What's my problem? First of all, I'm a rat." Remy goes on to describe his "highly developed sense of taste and smell," which leads to his fascination with cooking.

Remy's father, Django, is less than interested in Remy's abilities, valuing them only insofar as they help sniff out poisoned food. As the leader of the rat clan, Django is wary of humans and warns Remy to stay away from them. But Remy is fascinated by humans and their creativity, especially when it comes to food. Unwilling to tell his father about his desire to cook, Remy admits, "So now I had a secret life." Eventually Remy's secret life results in disaster for his rat colony when he and his brother, Emile, are discovered in a human kitchen and ultimately chased off at gunpoint. Later in the film, when Remy is reunited with his colony, his father expects him to stay permanently. "Maybe I'm a different kind of rat," Remy tells Django.

His father takes him to see what humans do to rats, showing him traps with dead rats in them. Remy is duly shocked but still refuses to believe that humans are all bad. "We look out for our own kind, Remy," says his father. "No," Remy replies. "No. Dad, I don't believe it. You're telling me that the future is—can only be—more of this." Django remarks, "This is the way things are. You can't change nature." But Remy still won't give in. "Change *is* nature, Dad—the part that we can influence. And it starts when we decide." Remy thinks he can move forward, literally and figuratively, when it comes to interactions with humans. His identity will always be that of a rat, but the choices he makes help shape, refine and hopefully improve his character and also his identity.

Identity and the Meaning of Life

Identity is important, but knowing who we are is not enough. Within the framework of God's calling, we need to act on our identity in order to make a meaningful moral difference in our lives as well as the lives of others. When Buzz Lightyear realizes he is a toy, rather than being encouraged and spurred to positive action, he becomes dejected and loses hope. In *Toy Story 2*, Woody already knows that his identity is that of a toy, but for a time he acts in a manner that goes against his purpose and identity. In *Ratatouille*, Remy too has to struggle with his identity and with those who oppose his desire to get along with humans. His confidence and desire to cook overcome his natural identity as a rat; he hopes that despite his identity as a rat, he can also, as he puts it, "add something to this world."

Understanding our true identity is foundational to living within God's calling. We can, of course, push back and decide to go our own way rather than God's way. Some do. The unfortunate consequences may not be readily apparent, but such a choice can disfigure the soul and neutralize our ability to make an eternal difference in God's kingdom. How do we avoid this potential pitfall? By continuously seeking first the kingdom of God and his righteousness (Matthew 6:33). Each of us will get off track at times. The good news is that, by God's grace and with Christ's help, we can always get back on.

Identity relates to the meaning of life. As Christians, our purpose is rooted in God and his nature. Christ is our example to follow. No, we won't be exactly like him, but we can try to emulate his virtues and strive to become who God would like us to be. In John 8:14, Jesus offered an example of the power of identity in relation to a life filled with purpose: "I know where I came from and where I am going," he said to the hypocritical leaders questioning him. His purpose and identity were perfectly clear to him and, as a result, his calling fell into place. This was true even though Christ's calling was not all pleasant and had a large share of pain and suffering. When given a firm foundation in Christ, identity helps us grow in relation to virtues such as friendship, courage, love and justice.

With the Christian life comes meaning, purpose and real identity. Knowing who we are, both as individuals and in Christ, will help us along as we face challenges. But we must actively seek to grow in Christ. The world is full of pretense—false concepts of identity that mask reality and, by doing so, obscure truth. We will face these pretenses both internally, in our thoughts, and externally, in the way the world around us functions. In such instances, a firm Christian identity is required.

Only then can we "take every thought captive to obey Christ" (2 Corinthians 10:5).

Discussion Questions

1. How does identity relate to the concept of being made in God's image?

2. Identity relates to calling, purpose, the meaning of life and even the formation of virtue. Give some examples of how some of these concepts are related.

3. Knowing our identity in Christ can help us make a positive difference in the world. How and why is this the case?

4. Buzz Lightyear has an identity crisis in *Toy Story;* in *Toy Story 2,* Woody has one. What's similar about their struggles with identity? What's different? How are their identity issues resolved?

5. How does knowing our identity and purpose help us grow in virtue and character?

JUSTICE

A Bug's Life—
"For oppressed ants everywhere!"

Flik means well. He really wants to help his ant colony out of an extremely difficult situation—one that he caused, albeit accidentally. Every year the ant colony works furiously to meet a deadline that requires them to gather large amounts of food for a gang of unruly grasshoppers led by Hopper, the meanest grasshopper of all. But this time Flik makes a mistake, and an invention he created to help speed along the food-gathering process inadvertently knocks the food offering into a pool of water. The grasshoppers are not pleased. Hopper demands twice as much food by the time they return, "when the last leaf falls." The colony blames Flik and brings him before a council for punishment. When he shares with the council his idea of leaving the colony to get help from bigger, tougher bugs, much to his surprise the council approves. Mostly they are glad to get rid of him.

Determined to help his colony, Flik sets out to seek assistance. Wearing a hat and carrying a sleeping pack on his back, both made out of green leaves, he departs the colony to great applause—not for his bravery, but because the colony is glad to see him go. A few ant children follow him, but two are not very supportive. One says that his dad expects Flik to be back within an hour, while another says his dad expects Flik will be killed. Only one ant, the young Princess Dot, encourages Flik.

As Flik reaches the edge of a deep canyon, his quest is momentarily halted. How will he get across? Thinking quickly, he climbs up a dandelion. As he plucks off a piece of it, he says, "Here I go. For the colony, and for oppressed ants everywhere!" Flik floats across the canyon, making it most of the way

ACTION!

A Bug's Life

U.S. Release Date: November 25, 1998

In order to capture the natural wonders seen from the perspective of ants, the Pixar team created what they called a "bug-cam." This miniature device had a camera attached to it that would film from an ant's point of view: what it was like for ants to crawl on the ground and look up at flowers, leaves, trees and other objects. John Lasseter, who directed the film, described the bug-cam footage as follows: "The one thing you noticed down at that level was how translucent everything was. To look up at a stalk of clover like it's a giant sequoia and see these huge clover leaves like giant stained-glass windows—it was stunning. The bugs have a beautiful view down there . . . it was breathtaking."[1] It's not just "the heavens" that "declare the glory of God" (Psalm 19:1 NIV), it's also the tiny natural world we walk across every day that does so.

before a breeze smashes him into a rock. Fortunately, the accident is not fatal and Flik continues his journey, eager to free his colony from the oppression of the grasshoppers. Ants must be freed and injustice corrected.

The Source of Justice

Justice on screen is not reserved only for courtroom dramas. Even computer-animated movies such as *A Bug's Life* can touch on the subject in unique ways. History is filled with references to justice, whether in the pages of philosophy, political writings, classic literature or other sources. In contemporary times the outcry for justice remains, though the foundations of its reality are more often than not blurred. What is justice? We know it when we see it, but usually we first see injustice in need of righting. In general terms, justice relates to fairness and equity. If someone is said to be "fair and reasonable," they might also be called "just." Justice spans the entire spectrum of human morality, meaning that it applies not only to what we would consider large matters, such as a murder trial, but also to what we might consider small matters, such as fairness in following the rules during a softball game. Justice also comes into play in relation to social ethics such as poverty, hunger and slavery.

Justice points to a moral foundation of right and wrong, but what is its source? The Christian position views justice as a cardinal virtue. Because we are human and made in God's image, part of the fabric of our being is morality, which includes justice. Like every true virtue, justice flows from God and his nature. In brief, God is the source of everything virtuous. The Bible refers to justice numerous times. In the New Testament, for example, the Golden Rule, as Christ shared, has justice as its foundation: "Whatever you wish that others would do to you, do also to them, for this is the Law and the Prophets" (Matthew 7:12). An alternate translation brings out the concepts of justice and fairness in relation to the passage in this manner: "In everything, therefore, treat people the same way you want them to treat you, for this is the Law and the Prophets" (NASB). The closing phrase of the passage is sometimes translated, "for this sums up the Law and the Prophets" (NIV). This phrase underscores the fact that justice is a foundational goal in the Old Testament, which contains "the Law and the Prophets," as well as in the New Testament.

This brings up another interesting point in relation to biblical views of justice: there is a difference between divine and human justice. Divine justice is perfect, for God makes no mistakes. Human justice, however, is imperfect. This does not mean that we should abandon our flawed efforts at pursuing justice, but rather that we should remain aware that the ideal goal of perfect justice is beyond our capabilities. Justice is connected to the holiness of God and, biblically, is often tied to righteousness. Justice and judgment, too, are connected, allowing us to better understand the theological doctrine of the atonement. Divine justice in relation to human sin, which has essentially broken our relationship with God, is restored only by way of the death of Christ. While several theories of the atonement attempt to explain exactly how God implemented divine justice in order to bring about restoration, all of them acknowledge that Christ's death is the key to this restoration.

Pixar's Justice

Although the topic of justice can easily lead to deep philosophical and theological discussions, everyone can relate on some level to justice. God placed a sense of morality, which includes an understanding of justice and injustice, in each of us. This is the reason that expressions of justice are found throughout popular culture and why the topic is of perennial interest to storytellers, including filmmakers. A sense of justice makes us cheer on the hero, whether on screen or in a book, as he or she overcomes injustices.

In Pixar's films, expressions of justice and fairness occur regularly. In *Toy Story*, the fact that the boy Sid is torturing toys is viewed by other toys as wrong and, in short, unjust. The moral center of justice, which seeks to set right that which is wrong, is also expressed in *Finding Nemo*, as Nemo seeks to avoid the injustice of being given away as a gift, which would separate him forever from his family. Two Pixar films in particular, though, are of special interest in relation to justice: *A Bug's Life* and *The Incredibles*.

Justice Is My Sword

When Heimlich the caterpillar is playing the role of Little John in
A Bug's Life, he menacingly threatens a group of bullying flies with
the words "Justice is my sword and truth shall be my quiver!" The
scene is played for laughs, but underlying Heimlich's words is the
thread of justice that is woven throughout the film via the plight
of the ants and the grasshoppers. Inspired by a twist on Aesop's
fable about the ants and the grasshopper, Pixar created a world
wherein grasshoppers are represented as a gang of thugs out to get
an ant colony to gather food for them. In doing so, Pixar brought
to life a vibrant and colorful world inhabited by all sorts of creatures, including P. T. Flea who runs a circus, Dim the timid blue
dung beetle, Rosie the black widow, Francis the ladybug, the pill
bugs Tuck and Roll, and of course, a colony of ants bullied by Hopper and his grasshopper gang.

On one level, *A Bug's Life* is an enjoyable family film about believing in yourself and doing the right thing. On another level,
however, it addresses questions of justice by telling a story filled
with injustice, persecution and oppression bordering on slavery.
Does this sound a bit melodramatic? It may be, considering it's
just a movie about a bunch of bugs. The deeper point, however, is
that the vice of injustice demands the virtue of justice. And so, a
hero is born in Flik, a bungling member of the ant colony and
budding inventor who sets out to find warrior bugs to defend the
colony against the oppressive grasshoppers. Flik, though, is up
against the tyrant Hopper, a grasshopper with an attitude. Under
the guise of guaranteeing the "safety" of the ant colony, in reality
the thug is forcing the ants to provide a regular food offering. "It
seems to me that you ants are forgetting your place," he says early
in the film. "So let's double the order of food!"

Hopper is no fool. He knows that all it takes is one person (or
in this case an ant) to light the fires of revolution against oppression and injustice. So when a group of grasshoppers suggests they

forget about going back to the ant colony, Hopper reminds them of the one ant, Flik, who stood up to him. "Yeah, but we can forget about him," says one of the grasshoppers, while another adds, "It was just one ant!" Hopper plays along, showing the grasshoppers one grain: "Say, let's pretend this grain is a puny little ant!" As Hopper begins throwing individual grains at some grasshoppers, he asks them if it hurts. Of course not—it's just a grain. "How about this?" asks Hopper as he removes the stopper on a large bottle of grain. Hundreds of grains pour out, burying the three grasshoppers who suggested not returning to the ant colony. "You let one ant stand up to us, then they all might stand up!" exclaims Hopper, climbing on top of the grain pile. "Those puny little ants outnumber us a hundred to one and if they ever figure that out, there goes our way of life! It's not about food; it's about keeping those ants in line! That's why we're going back."

Later, when the grasshoppers have returned to the colony, Hopper's concerns about "one ant" standing up to them are realized. Despite being beaten and threatened, Flik has the courage to stand up to Hopper. "I'm the one you want!" says Flik. Hopper begins to humiliate Flik, calling him a piece of dirt, then lower than dirt: "You're an ant! Let this be a lesson to all you ants. Ideas are very dangerous things. You are mindless, soil-shoving losers, put on this earth to serve us!"

The weakened Flik disagrees. "You're wrong, Hopper. Ants are not meant to serve grasshoppers. I've seen these ants do great things and year after year they somehow manage to pick food for themselves and you. . . . Ants don't serve grasshoppers! It's you who need us! We're a lot stronger than you say we are—and you know it, don't you?" No longer willing to accept the injustice of the grasshoppers, and spurred on by Flik's speech, the ant colony and the circus bugs are angry and ready to set right what is wrong. "You ants stay back!" warns Hopper. But it's too late. The ant revolution has begun, and with it the downfall of the tyrant Hopper and his oppressive grasshopper gang. Injustice is ultimately corrected, and the ants are free.

Incredible Justice

It's not only ants who seek justice. In *The Incredibles,* justice is the virtue that motivates superheroes. *Supers,* as they are called, go about doing what we've come to expect from superheroes based on comic books and movies: fight crime, catch criminals, set right what is wrong, protect the people, stand up to super-villains and, in the process, save the world. Without a moral foundation, heroes would not exist, either on screen or in the real world. But a moral foundation does exist, resulting in incredible justice. Even after the "glory days" of fighting crime, Bob Parr, aka Mr. Incredible, is still fighting against injustice in his own way. Forced to live in hiding and to suppress his superhero identity, Bob now works for an insurance company that does everything in its power to deny claims. Bob is undaunted, surreptitiously offering advice and guidance to customers to help them navigate the bureaucracy. This is an example of an everyday sort of justice, with Bob doing his part to help others and correct injustice.

During a meeting with his boss, the aptly named Mr. Huph, Bob glances out the window and witnesses a mugging in an alley. His immediate moral impulse is to intervene, to offer help, to stop the injustice that is taking place right before his eyes: "That man out there, he needs help." But Mr. Huph has no interest in the mugging other than hoping their insurance company doesn't cover the victim. Bob is upset, and his anger toward the injustice that is taking place is growing. "He got away," mutters Bob, as he sees the mugger running off. Unfortunately, Bob's desire for justice and his anger get the best of him, and he takes it out on Mr. Huph, throwing him through several walls.

On a grander scale are the heroic efforts of Mr. Incredible, actively seeking justice despite the risks. When Mr. Incredible learns that his nemesis Syndrome has been systematically murdering Supers and is plotting to attack a city, the goal is clear: stop him. What Syndrome is doing is morally wrong and, as such, unjust. Mr. Incredible does not stop and say, "I am now going to express the virtue of justice by stopping the injustices of Syndrome," but that is clearly the underlying moral motivation.

Seek Justice

In Isaiah 1:16-17 we read, "Wash yourselves; make yourselves clean; remove the evil of your doings from before my eyes; cease to do evil, learn to do good; seek justice, correct oppression; bring justice to the fatherless, plead the widow's cause." To "seek justice" is our goal. Christ said "the weightier matters of the law" are "justice and mercy and faithfulness" (Matthew 23:23). God requires of us justice, kindness and humility (Micah 6:8), not injustice, cruelty and pride.

Moreover, seeking justice may result in persecution and suffering. We are to pursue justice not because it is always easy—it's usually hard—but because it is right. Pursuing justice requires the virtue of courage and means taking real and meaningful moral action in a troubled world. A paraphrased version of the Golden Rule puts it well: "Here is a simple, rule-of-thumb guide for behavior: Ask yourself what you want people to do for you, then grab the initiative and do it for them. Add up God's Law and Prophets and this is what you get" (Matthew 7:12 *The Message*). In other words, seeking justice must move us to action, to actively make a positive moral difference. Injustice should upset us, as it upset Flik enough to do something about the oppression of Hopper and his gang of grasshoppers.

In seeking justice, however, we should not act unjustly ourselves, as Mr. Incredible did when he tossed Mr. Huph through some walls. Yes, muggers escape and injustice is not always set right, but that does not give us the right to behave unjustly in our search for justice. The mugging scene from *The Incredibles* illustrates another important principle, that is, when we do nothing to stop injustice, it spreads and becomes easier. Those who stand for justice must also stand against injustice.

Deep down inside, and sometimes not so deep down, we know about justice—even children do. Whenever a child in a playground calls out, "No fair!" that is an expression of justice that is morally inescapable. For the Christian, seeking justice is not an option. Instead, it is a foundational virtue.

Writing about justice is simpler than living it. On paper, justice seems easy enough. When situations call for it, we make the choice to do what is just, fair and right. Justice on screen seems easy enough too, especially when the situation involves computer-generated characters like Flik. In reality, more often than not justice is difficult. We live in a harsh world, where virtue is often trampled. This fact, however, should not discourage us, but encourage us to action. Needs in the area of social justice, for instance, should move us to real and meaningful moral interaction with our community and indeed the world. By ourselves we cannot right every wrong, but that shouldn't stop us from making a positive difference, even if on a small scale, whenever and wherever we can.

Discussion Questions

1. What ideas come to mind when you think of the term *justice?* In thinking about everyday life, where do you see justice and injustice taking place? Is there anything you can do about it?

2. How is justice a virtue? Why is injustice viewed as being wrong?

3. While *A Bug's Life* is about ants being bullied by grasshoppers, it says much about justice, injustice and oppression. What his-

torical and contemporary examples of similar forms of injustice can you recall? What are groups and individuals doing about these injustices? What can you do?

4. We're not superheroes, so we probably won't have to face supervillains like Syndrome, but what can you do in your daily life to make a difference in favor of justice?

5

FRIENDSHIP

Toy Story 2—
"You've got a friend in me."

A timid little penguin bounds into the scene, squeaking with every bounce. Woody the cowboy doll asks him how he's doing and Wheezy replies, "I feel swell. In fact, I think I feel a song coming on!" A big-band, Vegas-inspired rendition of "You've Got a Friend in Me" begins to play while Wheezy sings—with the voice of Robert Goulet, no less. Although Randy Newman's song is key to the original *Toy Story*, its role in *Toy Story 2* is even more powerful in communicating a message of friendship—a foundational virtue in Pixar films and in ethics.

Despite a daring rescue attempt by his friends, Woody, who has been taken by toy aficionado Al, chooses to stay behind in order to be part of a toy collection in a Japanese museum. In *Toy Story*, "You've Got a Friend in Me" served to establish the friendship between Woody and his owner, Andy, and later underscored the friendship between Buzz Lightyear and Woody. In *Toy Story 2* the song also serves a dual role, highlighting the friendship between the toys and reminding Woody of his friendship with Andy. As Buzz and the other toys leave Woody behind, Woody watches a scene from *Woody's Roundup* featuring an acoustic guitar version of "You've Got a Friend in Me," performed by a Woody puppet. "The real treasures are your friends and family," says the puppet. As Woody watches the song being performed, he rubs paint off the bottom of his boot, revealing the word "ANDY" (complete with a backwards *N*) and is reminded of his friendship with Andy, as well as his

ACTION!

Toy Story 2
U.S. Release Date: November 24, 1999

Originally intended as a direct-to-video sequel, *Toy Story 2* was produced in tandem with *A Bug's Life*, but with a smaller team, at a lower cost and somewhat rushed. Deemed acceptable but not exceptional, the Pixar team made the radical decision to significantly rethink the project well into the movie-making process, telling Disney that the film needed a restart in the production process. Pixar also said they wanted *Toy Story 2* released as a feature film. With only about nine months to go until the movie needed to be completed, Pixar's commitment to quality won out, and in the end *Toy Story 2* ended up being a superb film.

identity and purpose as a toy. His change of heart is immediate, and he decides to return to Andy. Friendship is more important than standing behind glass in a toy museum.

Our Friendship Will Never Die

On some level, we all understand what *friendship* means, but on another level, a successful definition eludes us. Is friendship a virtue? Ideally, it should be, but like so many other virtues, friendship is often fleeting, superficial and even twisted into forms that are less than virtuous. We live in a world of online social networking where we can instantly become someone's "friend" (see chapter eleven), and where degrees of friendship abound. Despite the haziness of the definition, however, there's no doubt that much of the happiness we experience in life is due to friendship.

But what is friendship? It is valued, sought after, enjoyed and maintained, sometimes over the course of a lifetime. When we know we have made a friend, on some level we experience joy. Deep and meaningful relationships all require friendship. Sometimes these relationships bring opposites together merely through the fact that the opposites share a common joy. In *Up*, the young and shy Carl Fredricksen, who will grow up to become a grumpy old man, has a passion for adventure and for his hero, Charles Muntz (see chapter nine for a discussion of adventure). Carl stumbles upon the clubhouse of Ellie, a talkative extrovert who shares Carl's love of adventure and of daring explorer Muntz. Two very different people—Carl and Ellie—are thus brought together as they share the joys of something they both love. Their friendship becomes deeper, turns to romantic love and then to a more mature love. And yet, the pattern begins with friendship.

Friendship and Love

Biblically speaking, friendship has its foundation in love. In the New Testament, the word often used for friendship is *philia*, while the term for fellowship, a form of friendship, is *koinonia*. In one sense, biblical friendship is no different from other forms of friendship. Friends spend time together, share common joys, talk with one another about what is meaningful, and offer support and advice. The key difference in Christian friendship is that God is the foundation of friendship, as he is so often the foundation of other virtues. While some forms of belief see a chasm so great between God and human beings so as to allow no friendship whatsoever between them, Christianity acknowledges a level of friendship between humans and God. But being friends with God is not the same as being friends with fellow humans. Friendship with God is conditional on our obedience.

Christ, moreover, equates friendship with sacrifice when he says, "Greater love has no one than this, that someone lay down his life for his friends" (John 15:13). The supreme sacrificial example of Christ—dying on the cross—is an example of godly friendship founded on God's love for us. While Pixar films are absent of such theological insights into divine friendship, they do include many meaningful examples of friendship.

Pixar's Friendships

In *WALL-E*, a garbage-compacting robot is friends with an indestructible cockroach. In *Ratatouille*, a rat is a friend to a human. In *Up*, a disillusioned old man learns to be a friend to an eager boy. Pixar revels in portraying unexpected friendships. Perhaps this is merely a storytelling method to make films more interesting, but maybe there is more to it. Do we tend to seek and maintain only the sorts of friendships that seem comfortable and expected, rather than those that might make us uncomfortable and are unexpected?

In the four New Testament Gospels, what example does Christ set for us in relation to friendships? Did he do what was expected, comfortable and ordinary, or did he color outside the lines of typical expectations of friendship? Even a cursory reading of the Gospels reveals Christ's eclectic friendships. Men, women, children, criminals, fishermen, tax collectors, prostitutes, Samaritans, Pharisees, "sinners": Christ befriended them all, reaching out to them with God's love.

Christ's friendships were unexpected, at least from the world's perspective. So, too, are some of the friendships found in Pixar films. In *Cars*, Piston Cup race car Lightning McQueen literally lives life in the fast lane. His purpose in life is to win races, not to cultivate friendships. He briefly realizes this when his agent offers him twenty free tickets to a race to pass on to friends. McQueen pauses, unable to think of anyone. It is only through a series of mishaps that McQueen ends up in Radiator Springs, a forgotten town off Route 66. The adventures he finds there lead him into an unexpected friendship with a rusty, dilapidated tow truck named Mater, who eventually becomes his best friend. The "odd couple" pairing of McQueen and Mater leads to friendship—something McQueen lacked despite his success on the racetrack.

Monsters and Friends

James P. Sullivan ("Sulley") and Mike Wazowski are best friends. They are just two everyday blue-collar workers who spend their days in a power plant. They're also monsters. Sulley is an enormous, blue-furred creature with horns on his head, while Mike is a small, green, one-eyed ball of energy. In *Monsters, Inc.*, it's their job to scare children in order to capture the power of screams.

In Sulley and Mike, Pixar once again manages to take strange characters, place them in situations everyone can relate to and craft a believable and emotionally powerful story. Throughout the film we learn bits and pieces of information about the two monsters. We know they are coworkers and roommates, that they went to school together since at least the fourth grade and that they are both intent on breaking the all-time scare record at their factory, Monsters, Incorporated.

As in any meaningful friendship, Sulley and Mike don't always get along. In *Monsters, Inc.*, friction arises when they find a human child—a little girl nicknamed Boo. In their world children are considered toxic, so the monsters are all afraid of kids. Uncertain what to do about the situation, Sulley and Mike smuggle Boo back to their apartment, where Sulley begins to understand that children aren't really toxic. At a key point in the film, Sulley and Mike are banished to the Himalayas in the middle of a blizzard. It is there that their friendship faces a real test. Sulley's only concern is to help Boo return to her own world safely, but Mike is distraught over being banished. They are found by another banished monster, the abominable snowman, but the tension between Sulley and Mike continues, even though the amusing abominable snowman recognizes that the two are best friends.

Mike doesn't budge. He's angry about being banished, is not interested in helping Boo and regrets being so close to breaking the scare record only to be sidetracked by Sulley. "None of that matters now," says Sulley. Mike is shocked and hurt. "What about me?" asks Mike. "I'm your pal, I'm your best friend—don't I matter?" Although Sulley apologizes, he turns again to the topic of helping Boo. Mike refuses to leave with Sulley, who is eager to find his way to a village in order to return to Monsters, Incorporated, through a closet in a child's bedroom. "You're on your own," says Mike, literally and figuratively turning his back on his best friend. Sulley leaves, intent on reaching the village by using a sled to speed his approach.

The reconciliation between Mike and Sulley takes place a short while later, though under confusing circumstances. Sulley has managed to rescue Boo from a despicable machine called the "scream extractor," but is now being pursued by the mean-spirited Randall, a purple lizard monster who is able to vanish by camouflaging himself within his surroundings. As an invisible Randall is attacking Sulley, Mike suddenly appears, tossing a snowball, and begins to apologize to Sulley. "You and I are a team," he says, "Nothing is more important than our friendship. . . . I'm sorry I wasn't there for you, but I am now." Friendship lost is now friendship restored.

Friendship and Moral Goodness

What can two monsters teach us about friendship? To begin, we learn that true friendship is indeed virtuous, and that friendship itself contains a certain moral goodness. As Christian ethics is rooted in God's love, so too is friendship. We also learn that friends need not be alike but may indeed be different, each one contributing to the friendship their own unique traits, for better or for worse. Friends also share common interests, whether it is their work, their hobbies or other things. Friendship brings about joys that are greater when shared than when alone.

Sulley and Mike also demonstrate the reality of friction in friendships. The truth is that we live in a fallen world made up of fallen creatures. Given the reality of human depravity, friction is inevitable, even among friends. But the reality of tensions within friendships should not deter us from pursuing friendships. Rather, overcoming challenges in friendships will help us grow morally, thus helping us become better individuals. Reconciliation is also important in friendship, as it requires us to actively participate in and understand restoration. What is involved in reconciliation? There needs to be repentance—a sincere turning away from whatever it was that resulted in tension and division to begin with. Repentance also requires humility—the opposite of pride. In sum, tensions in friendship that require reconciliation help us grow virtuously as individuals.

What about reconciliation between ourselves and God? Romans 5:10-11 reads, "For if while we were enemies we were reconciled to God by the death of his Son, much more, now that we are reconciled, shall we be saved by his life. More than that, we also rejoice in God through our Lord Jesus Christ, through whom we have now received reconciliation." Moreover, Christian reconciliation is also tied to holiness: "And you, who once were alienated and hostile in mind, doing evil deeds, he [Christ] has now reconciled in his body of flesh by his death, in order to present you holy and blameless and above reproach before him" (Colossians 1:21-22).

The closing credits song of *Monsters, Inc.*—Randy Newman's "If I Didn't Have You"—reiterates the value of friendship, particularly with repeated words underscoring the need for meaningful friendships. What would we have if we did not have harmony between ourselves and God? Are we "friends" with God? In John 15:14-15, Jesus said, "You are my friends if you do what I command you. No longer do I call you servants, for the servant does not know what his master is doing; but I have called you friends, for all that I have heard from my Father I have made known to you." Of course, friendship with God is, as we have noted, not identical to friendships among ourselves. God is perfectly holy, while we are not. God is complete in and of himself, while we are dependent on him; therefore we should have a good deal of reverence toward our Creator. Jesus goes on to say in verse 17, "These things I command you, so that you will love one another." The goal of his command, then, is not some sort of domineering control over us, but a desire to see us love others genuinely. But first we must love God (Matthew 22:36-39).

The Clown and the Angel

Another Pixar example of an unusual friendship involves Marlin and Dory in *Finding Nemo*. Marlin is a nervous, overprotective clownfish searching for his son, Nemo, while Dory is a playful, adventurous blue angelfish with memory problems. While searching for his son, Marlin runs into Dory. The two are first traveling companions by utility—Dory says she has seen a boat and, later, is able to help Marlin decipher the name and address on a diving mask that he believes will lead him to Nemo. Upon their first meeting, Marlin is puzzled, noticing Dory's strange behavior. "Something's wrong with you," he tells her, adding, "You're wasting my time."

After meeting up with a few sharks and deciphering the writing on the diving mask, Marlin is more than happy to now shed the sometimes bothersome Dory. He has the information he needs and, in his assessment, Dory is a "delay fish." Dory is saddened but not deterred. Together, they press on in search of Nemo.

Dory's friendship with Marlin is an interesting one. In having to address her childlike behavior, Marlin is in some ways learning to be a better father. His encounter with a group of sea turtles also helps him along, as do his other adventures on his journey to find

Nemo. As Andrew Stanton, director of *Finding Nemo*, has stated, the film is essentially about the power of faith to overcome fear. Dory helps Marlin do this, not deliberately but just by being who she is—carefree and adventurous.

When Marlin thinks Nemo is dead, he is understandably upset. He thanks Dory for her help and then begins to leave her. Dory doesn't understand why he would leave. "Stop!" she calls out to him. "Please don't go away. Please. No one's ever stuck with me for so long before. . . . I look at you, and I'm home." Whatever her short-comings may be, Dory recognizes the value of a true friend. In the end, Marlin is not only a better parent but also a better friend.

A Theology of Friendship

Most of us probably don't think too much about a theology of friendship, but doing so will yield some beneficial results. For instance, the natural desire for friendship offers many insights into human nature. Why do we want and seek friendship? One reason is that we long for something in this world to offer fulfillment and joy in our lives. We may seek this fulfillment in materialism, by accumulating possessions, through hobbies, by occupying our time with diversions and other activities, and in some cases, through friendship. This does not diminish the inherent value of friendship, but it does indicate that we are missing something. In this sense, friendship points us to God.

Christian theology also offers an example of friendship as well as a foundation for love. Within the nature of the Trinity, Father, Son and Holy Spirit are involved in a dynamic interplay—one God revealed in three persons, united and complete. In 1 John 4:8 we read, "God is love," but Aelred of Rievaulx (1109–1166) paraphrased the passage as "God is friendship," thus emphasizing the relational aspects not only of God's love but of the very nature of friendship. In this sense, then, true friendship helps us move closer to God and to his desire for us to grow and mature spiritually.

A proper Christian theology of friendship encourages the cultivation of long-term, enduring friendships, meaning that they move beyond the superficial and into rich and meaningful interaction over a long period of time. Unfortunately, the contemporary world often makes it difficult to foster these kinds of friendships. More than ever before, the world is moving at metaphorically incredible speeds, as we travel at fast speeds, move from one area to another and perhaps live many miles from where we work. Often we no longer know what it means to be part of a community or how to build theologically healthy friendships. Even the term *friend* is diminished, skewing our perception of what friendship should be in a biblical sense. True friendship does not exist for the sake of personal gain of any kind, other than the natural virtuous "gain" of being friends. In other words, friendships that are solely utilitarian—that is, those that are forged only to be useful to us—are not true friendships.

We should not seek friendships merely for personal gain or as some sort of technique that we may use for our own purposes. True friendship helps us in some small way better understand the goodness of God. Moreover, it's easy for us to establish and maintain friendship only with those who are more like us than not. Doing so will result in Christians having primarily or perhaps even exclusively Christian friends. But as the example of Christ demonstrates, our friendships often need broadening. Moving beyond our comfort zones in friendship will provide opportunities to not only grow in character ourselves, but help others grow too.

Discussion Questions

1. What are some examples of friendship in *Toy Story 2?*

2. Mike and Sulley are best friends, but even so they face their share of difficulties. What sort of attitude is necessary to foster

reconciliation? How does Mike go about reconciling with Sulley?

3. What role does love play in a biblical view of friendship? How is God involved in friendship?

4. In what way are we friends with God? Discuss the meaning of Christ's sacrifice in relationship to love and friendship.

HUMOR

Monsters, Inc.—
"These are the jokes, kid."

The movie is over. Mike the upbeat, one-eyed green monster has finished rebuilding Boo's broken door for his best friend Sulley. Sulley, also a monster, places the last piece where it belongs, steps through the opening and is greeted by the joyful voice of a human child: "Kitty!" The credits begin to roll as we hear a duet of Randy Newman's "If I Didn't Have You," performed by Billy Crystal (Mike) and John Goodman (Sulley). So ends the Pixar film *Monsters, Inc.* Or does it?

About a month after the theatrical release of the film, Pixar added a series of animated outtakes to the end credits. Being a computer-generated movie, *Monsters, Inc.* didn't really have these bloopers, but that didn't stop Pixar from creatively putting together a series of humorous scenes complete with computer-animated characters, shots of boom mics getting in the way and other amusing outtakes we are used to seeing in relation to traditional live-action comedy films.

The outtakes include Sulley, the large furry blue monster, falling backwards over a chair as he fends off the "dangerous" human child nicknamed Boo. The next blooper features a shot of several "scarers" entering the "scare floor" at Monsters, Incorporated, looking very much like the classic scene in the film *The Right Stuff*, but with monsters instead of astronauts. But Sulley trips, which causes all the other monsters to fall too; so much for the majestic entrance. If that weren't enough, the serious monster character Roz, who is perpetually gloomy in the film, continues to show up in various outtakes, surprising and amusing the monster "actors." When a young worker accidentally refers to James Sullivan as Mr. Solomon, his coworker panics: "You idiot, it's 'Sullivan,' not 'Solomon.' You're messing up the scene! We're never gonna work in Hollywood again!" One outtake features an unexpected sight—Rex, the timid green dinosaur from the *Toy Story* films. This time Rex is apparently auditioning for the role of Ted, a giant monster. "Hey, how was that?" asks Rex, excitedly. "Was I scary? Do I get the part? Can I do it again? I can be taller."

The outtakes culminate in a musical, *Put That Thing Back Where It Came from or So Help Me!*, presented by the Monsters,

ACTION!

Monsters, Inc.

U.S. Release Date: November 2, 2001

All Pixar films feature great voices to go along with the amazing visuals. From Tom Hanks as Woody, the cowboy doll in the *Toy Story* movies, to Ed Asner's outstanding performance as Carl Fredricksen in *Up*, every Pixar movie includes distinctive voice talent. In the main roles for *Monsters, Inc.* are John Goodman as Sulley and Billy Crystal as Mike. Crystal had turned down the part of Buzz Lightyear in *Toy Story*, a role that ultimately went to Tim Allen. Describing his role as Mike, the one-eyed monster, Crystal has said, "Mike was an appealing, odd little guy who I thought was a combination of Mr. Toad and Sammy Davis, Jr. . . . [Mike] was one of my favorite characters that I've ever played."[1]

Inc. Company Players. Sulley introduces the play, complete with microphone feedback noises. A musical summary of the movie *Monsters, Inc.* ensues, featuring musical numbers performed by Billy Crystal as Mike, with gripping lyrics such as, "There's a child, there's a child, there's a human child! Running around the restaurant, this is really wild! What in heaven's name will become of us—we who are living in Monstropolis!" As the play concludes, Mike remarks, "What a night for my mother to be in the audience, ladies and gentlemen," whereupon we are treated to a glimpse of Mike's mother, who looks exactly like him except for the fact that she has red shoes, glasses (well, one lens, anyway), red lipstick and pointy blue hair. Obviously thrilled to be at her son's performance, she wears a novelty foam "#1" hand on her left hand.

Monsters, Inc. isn't the only Pixar film to feature amusing outtakes. The animation studio began the practice with the credits for *A Bug's Life* and also carried it into films such as *Toy Story 2*. The end credits of *Cars* doesn't feature outtakes per se, but it does contain additional scenes and, amusingly, drive-in movie clips of various Pixar films with uniquely automotive twists, including *Toy Car Story*, *Monster Trucks, Inc.* and *A Bug's Life* featuring a VW Bug playing the part of Flik the ant. Pixar also has the sense of humor to poke fun at itself by pointing out that one particular voice is featured repeatedly in its films, namely, that of John Ratzenberger, known for his recurring role as Cliff the mailman in the TV sitcom *Cheers*. "Wait a minute here," says Mack the truck from *Cars*, played by Ratzenberger, "They're just using the same actor over and over! What kind of a cut-rate production is this?"

Pixar Animation Studios definitely has a sense of humor. While this isn't the only reason Pixar films are successful, it is certainly a key factor. But how is humor tied to virtue? What is the relationship between humor and Christian theology? This chapter will seek to address these and related questions.

A Theology of Humor?

Humor is usually easy to recognize but not so easy to define. It relates to comedy or the comic, which is associated with laughter. When we laugh, it's usually because of something funny that creates joy in us. Joy is a feeling of unusual pleasure and is associated with happiness. Humor, then, encompasses many feelings, but all are expected to be positive and uplifting—unless we are discussing dark comedy, which takes serious subjects such as war and looks at them from a strangely humorous angle.

Not all humor is created equal, however. Like anything good, humor can be corrupted or spoiled, resulting in humor that is not God-honoring. When good humor is warped, it is no longer good. We may still find it amusing, but we must keep in mind that we are fallen beings in need of redemption. Our reactions to what we encounter in life are not perfect but are often marred by our own corrupt nature.

What about humor and the Bible? Is it possible to successfully construct what we might term a theology of humor? Ecclesiastes 3:4 reminds us that there is "a time to laugh," but we'll get no details out of the passage. Do we fare any better by examining other biblical passages related to humor? Many psalms reference the laughter of God. Psalm 2:4, for instance, reads, "He who sits in the heavens laughs." When we look at the context, however, we see that the passage is contrasting God with weak and rebellious human leaders. In this sense, the laughter of the passage is tied to ridicule. Note, too, that the Bible is filled with figurative language. In other words, the passage may simply be communicating to us in a way that we can relate to—someone laughing at the folly of another.

Psalm 37:13 provides us with another example of this sort of laughter—"the Lord laughs at the wicked"—as does Psalm 59:8. These passages deliberately attribute human qualities to God in order to get a point across in terms with which hearers can relate. This does not mean, however, that God does not have what we'd call a sense of humor. If we grant that there is such a thing as humor and that it is good, and if this sort of humor is rooted in God's nature, as are other virtues, then it stands to reason that some humor is good, and perhaps even godly and God-honoring.

If all the various Bible stories and genres were lumped into one broad category—no easy task—then it most certainly would not be comedy (although some Jewish scholars consider the book of Esther to be comedic). In fact, it probably would fit best under the category of drama or even of tragedy. At least, that's the thrust of much of the Bible as it relates to humans. The broad arc of the biblical story is that of good humanity gone wrong. God's actions in history are not only to restore the relationship that is severed with humans but also to restore creation. That's hardly comedic material. If humor is related to joy, however, then there is something to be said in favor of a theology of humor. The joys of laughter, for instance, can offer us glimpses of the future heavenly joy that awaits us.

What about humor in relation to Christ? The shortest verse in the Bible reads, "Jesus wept" (John 11:35), but we have no verse explicitly stating, "Jesus laughed." Unfortunately, Christianity is often portrayed as somber, for indeed it deals with serious issues. Christians themselves often communicate a level of seriousness that tends to suffocate any semblance of humor and joy in the Christian life. Nearly every film depicting the life of Jesus pictures him as a continuously serious individual. Why shouldn't he be? After all, he is calling people to repentance, not inviting them to a stand-up comedy routine.

But if we grant the theological position that Jesus was fully human and fully divine, then it stands to reason that in his human nature, he had a sense of humor. Granted, his sense of humor would not be warped by sin and the Fall, but he would have one nonetheless. The logical conclusion is not only that Jesus had a sense of humor but also that he laughed, thus expressing joy.

Did Jesus ever say anything funny? There is no laugh track accompanying the written record we know as the New Testament, but there are several indicators of Christ's humor. For example, many of the word pictures Jesus created in the minds of his listeners were certainly amusing: "You blind guides, straining out a gnat and swallowing a camel!" (Matthew 23:24); "Again I tell you, it is easier for a camel to go through the eye of a needle than for a rich person to enter the kingdom of God" (Matthew 19:24); "Why do you see the speck that is in your brother's eye, but do not notice the log that is in your own eye?" (Luke 6:41).

Elton Trueblood, author of the 1964 book *The Humor of Christ*, wrote,

> The widespread failure to recognize and to appreciate the humor of Christ is one of the most amazing aspects of the era named for Him. Anyone who reads the Synoptic Gospels [Matthew, Mark and Luke] with a relative freedom from presuppositions might be expected to see that Christ laughed, and that He expected others to laugh, but our capacity to miss this aspect of His life is phenomenal. We are so sure that He was always deadly serious that we often twist His words in order to try and make them conform to our preconceived mold. A misguided piety has made us fear that acceptance of His obvious wit and humor would somehow be mildly blasphemous or sacrilegious. Religion, we think, is serious business, and serious business is incompatible with banter.[2]

Trueblood is so convinced of the humor of Christ that he lists no less than thirty New Testament passages wherein Jesus offers some sort of humor.

Jesus had a keen wit and a subtle but powerful sense of irony. He often created amusing word pictures via parables, and he also used a form of logical argumentation known as reductio ad absurdum, whereby an opponent's position is exposed as absurd, sometimes humorously.

Pixar's Humor

Pixar's humor runs throughout its films. In *A Bug's Life*, Hopper is amused by the antics of the circus bugs' performance, particularly when the pill bugs, Tuck and Roll, sing and dance and then begin to argue and repeatedly slap and push one another. "Now that's funny," remarks Hopper; "I guess we could use a little entertainment."

Toy Story 2 includes its share of humor as well. The opening sequence featuring Buzz Lightyear on a dangerous mission is one example. At one point Buzz is surrounded by enemy robots, agents of his archenemy Zurg, all of whom aim their weapons at him and cover him with little red dots of light. The robots are then shown close up, with smaller robots wielding weapons springing from their shoulders, and the newly appearing smaller robots also have smaller gun-wielding robots springing from their shoulders. Later when Woody is watching the television show *Woody's Roundup*, a group of woodland creatures arrives in a desperate effort to get help to Jessie and Prospector, who are trapped in a mine. The animals barely have time to make a few critter noises when Woody replies, knowingly and quite rapidly, "What's that? Jessie and Prospector are trapped in the old abandoned mine and Prospector just lit a stick of dynamite thinking it was a candle and now they are about to be blown to smithereens?" A rabbit nods in reply: "Mm, hm."

The Incredibles also includes its share of humor, particularly when it comes to the French villain, Bomb Voyage, who wears a beret, has his face painted like a mime and makes snide remarks in French. Another hilarious scene occurs when Mr. Incredible's back goes out in the middle of a fight with an Omnidroid robot prototype.

There's also a highly amusing scene in *Up*. As the "camera" shifts to three tough dogs in the South American jungle, one in particular is more ominous than the others. It is a sleek black doberman, sitting quietly and ominously staring out into the jungle. This is not ordinary dog, however. His master, famous explorer Charles Muntz, has fitted him with a collar that allows the dog to speak. As the camera slowly pans in to the Doberman, he begins to talk. The expectation is for a deep, threatening voice to emanate from the speaker on his collar. Instead, viewers are treated to the high-pitched voice of the dog, Alpha, because his collar is broken. He sounds as though he has just sucked some helium. The scene is hilarious, resulting in many laughs from viewers. Throughout the film, Alpha's broken collar provides many moments of comic amusement.

While many Pixar films are filled with laughs, this section will focus on *Monsters, Inc.*, *Ratatouille* and *WALL-E*.

Make Her Laugh!

We've already noted the humorous outtakes featured during the end credits of *Monsters, Inc.*, but there's more to this story. The overarching plot of *Monsters, Inc.* is about monsters who need to scare children in order to capture their screams, which in turn provide power and electricity to the monster world. The storytelling concept of reversal is obviously at play here: normally children are afraid of monsters, but in *Monsters, Inc.*, it is monsters who are afraid of children. This provides for many humorous scenes involving the human child, nicknamed Boo, scaring monsters rather than being scared by them.

Throughout the film, strange things happen when Boo laughs: lights flicker on and off more than once, and in one instance the power grid is overloaded and causes a blackout. Although it takes some time for him to figure it out, eventually the large furry monster Sulley realizes that Boo's laughter generates incredible amounts of power. At one point while Mike and Sulley are evading the evil Randall, they need to get power to some doors that act as portals in the monster world. They need to do it quickly, so that they can escape through the doors when they are activated. Sulley encourages Mike to make Boo laugh, thus providing power to the doors. "Make her laugh! Just do it!" Mike slaps his own eye, Boo laughs and the doors receive enough power to open. Upon finding Boo's door to her own room, the power is out again. "Make her laugh again," says Sulley. Arms crossed, Boo awaits something funny. Mike squeezes his head in a door, but Boo does not laugh. "These are the jokes, kid," he says grumpily.

In the end, the fiendish plan to extract screams from children by force is exposed. Many think that Monsters, Incorporated, will shut down as a result, but Sulley has a great idea. Instead of scaring children, why not make them laugh to generate power? No longer is the company motto, "We scare because we care," valid. Sulley transforms Monsters, Incorporated, into a place of laughter and joy. Now monsters do not sneak into children's rooms to scare them but to make the kids laugh. Mike does a stand-up comedy routine, while other monsters perform various acts in order to capture laughter. The "scare floor" is now the "laugh floor," and a festive, party-like atmosphere fills the company, complete with streamers, colorful balloons and banners that read, "THINK FUNNY." Sulley notes that "laughter is ten times more powerful than scream." Better to jump with joy than be filled with fear.

Of Rats and Robots

Ratatouille and *WALL-E* both offer their share of humor too. The former is about a rat named Remy who aspires to be a chef, while the latter is about a robot, WALL-E, and his love for the robot EVE, the Extraterrestrial Vegetation Evaluator. But the humor in *Ratatouille* and *WALL-E* is largely about ideas and visual gags. *Ratatouille* is amusing because no one expects a rat to become a renowned chef, much less control a clumsy human, Alfredo Linguini, by pulling on locks of hair on his head. At one point, after a hard night's work, Linguini is asleep on the floor of the kitchen of Gusteau's restaurant. Remy the rat arrives and notices that another employee, Colette, is about to enter the building. Linguini happens to like Colette, but he is shy and awkward. Remy crawls under Linguini's chef's hat. Unable to awaken Linguini, Remy places sunglasses on the slumbering human and hopes to control his actions, thereby convincing Colette that Linguini is awake and working. Colette walks in only to see a bored-looking Linguini scrubbing a pan. She speaks to him, but Remy is only able to make Linguini nod. Colette is hurt that Linguini will not respond to her: "I thought you were different. I thought you thought I was different. I thought . . ." Linguini's head flops over and he snores.

WALL-E is also humorous, while at the same time it presents viewers with challenging ideas about technology and our use of it (see chapter eleven). But in many respects, WALL-E is akin to a silent movie. There are long stretches during which there is no dialogue at all—just visuals, sound effects and, at times, music. The audience is treated to an uplifting song from Hello, Dolly! early on and later watches the daily routine of WALL-E, the grubby, garbage-compacting robot, as he goes about collecting oddities like a rubber duck and paddle ball and trying out a bra on his mechanical eyes. When he finds a jewelry case containing a large diamond he is audibly pleased, but quickly proceeds to toss away the diamond while keeping the velvet box, intrigued by the hinge mechanism. WALL-E also learns how to use a fire extinguisher as a propulsion device, shooting himself around—a technique that proves useful when he ends up in space with nothing but a fire extinguisher to control his movements.

More humor ensues after the robot EVE arrives looking for plant life. When she finds it, she shuts down and WALL-E, who has a certain affection for her, is concerned and takes care of her.

While upbeat music plays, WALL-E tries to shield EVE from rain during a storm only to be struck by lightning. When the little robot tries to jump-start EVE, the shock sends him flying. Later he wraps Christmas lights around EVE and, while sitting on a bench watching the sunset, he tries to hold her "hand," which closes forcefully on WALL-E. When he's bored, we see WALL-E playing the old video game *Pong* (he's winning, 8,000 to 0).

Ratatouille and *WALL-E* are both clever in relation to humor. They take viewers' preconceived expectations and turn them on their heads. They also provide viewers with rich visual humor that in many ways is more difficult to pull off than humor that is based on words such as jokes. There is a certain amount of joy and delight in the films, too. Remy loves to cook, and doing so makes him happy. WALL-E is childlike in his innocence, a quality that often causes inadvertent humor.

Humor, Virtue and Joy

Pixar films are funny—not continuously so, but the humor is peppered throughout. We enjoy watching them because they are humorous, entertaining and, as a whole, contain positive messages for families. But how does humor relate to virtue? Perhaps more importantly, how does humor relate to us on a practical, day-to-day level? Humor is virtuous insofar as it is grounded in the delight and joy that is rooted in God. Instead of pursuing entertainment solely for the purposes of diversion or to take our minds off unhappiness or other challenges, we should try to see humor redemptively. What is it that underlies good humor? It is a sense of delight. In addition, humor often succeeds when it makes fun of vice, whether it be pride, gluttony, envy, sloth, etc. By doing so, we should look at the other side of vice and turn toward virtue. Let us also seek to turn the lens of humor on ourselves. Being what we are—fallen human beings—we often try to justify less-than-acceptable thoughts, words and behavior. If we take a moment to reflect on the futility of self-justification and our efforts to save ourselves, we can begin to look toward the true source of our justification: God through Christ.

Humor also offers Christians glimpses of the joy that awaits us. In Revelation, the reuniting of God's people with him is compared to the celebration of a wedding feast, full of rejoicing (Revelation 19:7-9; 21). Our heavenly hope is real, as is the laughter that will undoubtedly accompany the celebratory occasion. Psalm 32:11 reads, "Be glad in the LORD and rejoice, O righteous, and shout for joy, all you upright in heart." Seeking virtue is not intended to get us down but to lift us up. As we function within the joyful parameters God has created for us, we grow in joy. This does not mean that there are no times for seriousness, because Christianity indeed offers a somber message to humanity. This message ends in good news, however, through the gospel of Christ and what he has done for us. The Christian life is not supposed to be stuffy and boring. God delights in us and perhaps even laughs at us too. To be fully human, we need to laugh.

Pixar films succeed, at least in part, because of humor. If we try to remain serious all the time, our lives will remain dull and lifeless rather than vibrant and joyful. This is not to say that joy and laughter are exclusive to our emotional range (they aren't), but to keep in mind that they have their place. The sober-minded author of Ecclesiastes reminds us that there is "a time to laugh" (3:4) even when there is also "a time to weep." The virtues of humor are undergirded by joy and delight, which are established in God.

Discussion Questions

1. Think of one of your favorite Pixar movies or characters. What makes the movie or character funny to you?

2. Most of us have not spent any significant time developing a theology of humor. What do you think of humor and joy in re-

lation to God the Father and Christ the Son? Can you think of any biblical examples that are suggestive of humor?

3. If you have seen *Ratatouille* or *WALL-E*, name a couple of instances of humor in those films. What about those scenes did you find funny? Why?

4. How might Christians view humor redemptively?

FAMILY

Finding Nemo— "I have to find my son!"

An eager young couple is admiring the breathtaking view from their new home. Everything they need to raise a family is available to them—a wonderful neighborhood, great schools and their new home. The adventure of life is open before them. Understandably, they want the best for their children.

This story could be told of countless families, but what makes it unusual in this case is that it is about two clownfish, Marlin and Coral, in the film *Finding Nemo*. Pixar's stories may be set in fanciful worlds featuring talking fish, but they resonate with us not because of their fantastic elements but because of the elements to which we can relate: family, friendship, love and, in the case of parents, the sincere desire for the best for their children.

But something goes wrong, as so often does not only in films but in life. The world is beautiful and full of possibilities, but it's also dangerous and fraught with pitfalls. As Marlin and Coral are enjoying their anticipation of parenthood, their undersea joy is shockingly interrupted by a vicious barracuda attack. In his efforts to defend his family, Marlin is knocked unconscious, landing in his anemone home. When he awakens, he finds that his wife, Coral, is gone, as are all their eggs—all, that is, except one. Marlin lovingly holds the egg in his fins, naming the sole survivor "Nemo" in accordance with Coral's wishes. From death and devastation, Marlin finds new life and is intent on protecting his son at all costs. "I promise," says Marlin, "I will never let anything happen to you . . . Nemo."

ACTION!

Finding Nemo

U.S. Release Date: May 30, 2003

True to the immersive research Pixar's filmmakers put into every project, while working on *Finding Nemo* they brought in a large aquarium (fully stocked with saltwater fish), and members of the movie team went scuba diving in order to gain firsthand experience of the ocean world. An undersea expert was hired to field questions and consult on the film. The result is a computer-generated movie featuring many accurate depictions of sea life, with some room for creative license (for instance, fish that talk).

Finding Nemo is, at its heart, all about family. A widowed, single parent wants the best for his son. Having experienced tragedy, Marlin becomes so overprotective that he smothers and stifles Nemo, a young clownfish with a gimpy fin. But Marlin means well. He's seen what the dangerous world can do.

Pixar films bring home both the joys and challenges of families. The location and characters in the stories Pixar tells vary: *Finding Nemo* takes us on an undersea adventure, while *The Incredibles* is about a family of superheroes struggling to fit into a world that has left little room for them. Yet they face challenges we can relate to—sibling rivalry, employment that is not always satisfying, problems with school, strains on marriage. In *Up*, Pixar also reveals insights into family, this time by way of a quiet and reserved young man named Carl Fredricksen who marries his childhood sweetheart, Ellie. Along the way, Carl and Ellie face many struggles, as do most families. But in the end, their love is worth everything they have been through.

It's Complicated—It's Family

Addressing the topic of family is not easy. As the gifted chef Remy the rat explains in *Ratatouille*, to the point of exasperation, "It's complicated, it's—it's family." Whether we are married, single, have children or not, we are all part of a family. But what is a family? Moreover, what is a biblical view of the family? What about parenting? Is there some technique that will help every parent succeed?

While contemporary Western culture has in many ways stretched the definition of family in more ways than can be counted, at some level we know what family means. There is, of course, the traditional family, consisting of a mother, father and one or more children. For some, family brings to mind joyful memories, while for others family is not so pleasant. A family forms a household which, in turn, is a societal unit. Ideally, home is where many positive things should take place, including moral development. But no family is perfect. It is, in fact, this imperfection in families that drives many aspects of storytelling, including Pixar films.

Biblically speaking, family is often used metaphorically in order to clarify important theological truths. The godhead, for instance, consists of Father, Son and Holy Spirit, coexisting in love and unity and, to a certain extent, is illustrative of family. Consider, for instance the terms *Father* and *Son*—deliberately chosen by God to help us relate to a basic family structure. There's also an application to the Christian church family or body. Fellow Christians, though they may not be biologically related, are said to be brothers and sisters in Christ. We're also said to be "children of God" (see, for instance, John 1:12; Romans 8:21; Philippians 2:15; 1 John 3:1-2).

Moreover, the concept of covenant comes into play in relation to family. As God has had covenant dealings with humans, so too does the family unit constitute a covenant—that is, a relational agreement with certain expectations and parameters. Being in a covenant family helps prepare each of us for the realities and challenges we will face as we mature, helping us grow in virtue. Is family a virtue? In and of itself that's not necessarily the case, but family doesn't exist in a vacuum. Families are places where virtues such as love should exist, as well as aspects of identity and friendship. Family may also help us accept biblical concepts such as unconditional acceptance and love.

Pixar's Families

Pixar's films make no efforts to deliberately portray a distinctly Christian family. Instead, they seek to illustrate the typical trials and challenges that most families face. This does not mean, however, that the wisdom Pixar offers in relation to families is useless. On the contrary, it is of utmost value. *Toy Story* and *Toy Story 2* are primarily about toys, but families are included. The boy, Andy, has a younger sister, Molly, and they are cared for by their seemingly single-parent mother (we are not told details regarding the whereabouts of or situation with the father). In *Toy Story*, the troubled neighbor boy, Sid, lives with his parents and sister, but in some degree of neglect. Three other Pixar films, however, will be the focus of our attention here: *Finding Nemo, The Incredibles* and *Up*.

A Fish Can Breathe Out Here

Along with *The Incredibles, Finding Nemo* overtly addresses family-related themes, especially parenting and the parent-child relationship. As we've read at the beginning of this chapter, *Finding Nemo* starts with an eager young couple, Marlin and Coral, getting ready to embark on the adventure of parenthood. Marlin is delighted with the home they have acquired; "A fish can breathe out here," he says. But soon their dreams are shattered, and Marlin is the lone parent to the surviving egg, Nemo. Marlin deals with common parental concerns such as dropping a child off at school for the first time—although in Marlin's case, the concerns are magnified by his paranoia. Even before Nemo is born, Marlin expresses his insecurities about being a parent. "What if they don't like me?" he asks Coral. Whenever Nemo is even remotely in any danger, Marlin is there to take care of everything. When a scuba diver captures Nemo, Marlin is willing to do anything to get his son back. The result is an incredible odyssey for both Marlin and Nemo, and, ironically, separately they learn more about being together.

When Marlin gains a companion in Dory, the fish with memory problems, together the search for Nemo continues. Perhaps some of the clearest parental lessons Marlin learns on his journey take place when he encounters a large group of sea turtles traveling on the East Australian Current. The wound-up, overprotective Marlin meets the laid-back sea turtle Crush, who represents almost the opposite of Marlin's parenting style. When one of Crush's children, Squirt, is pulled out of the current, Marlin is quick to panic and anxious to go after him, but Crush knows better. "Whoa, kill the motor, dude," says Crush. "Let us see what Squirt does flying solo." Sure enough, Squirt returns on his own, excited about what he has done, allowing for an opportunity to bond with Crush rather than be punished or fretted over. After word travels of Marlin's adventures and finally reaches Nemo by way of Nigel the pelican, Nemo is filled with pride in his father. He understands something about how much his father loves him and the lengths he will go to get Nemo back.

When Marlin and Dory are swallowed by a whale, another opportunity for Marlin to grow as a parent presents itself. He is trapped, unable to continue his journey, and faces a crisis of faith. No matter how hard he tries, he can't escape. While Marlin relentlessly smashes against the sides of the whale, determined to escape and continue his search for Nemo, Dory is casually swimming around, delighted by the experience. Marlin is on the verge of panic: "I have to get out! I have to find my son! I have to tell him how old sea turtles are!" What is touching about the scene is the incredible power of parental love displayed by Marlin. All he wants is to continue the search for his son. Dory tries to console Marlin, who has nearly given up hope. "It'll be okay," she says. "No, no it won't," says Marlin. "I promised him I would never let anything happen to him." Dory points out the absurdity of this promise: "That's a funny thing to promise. You can't never let anything happen to him; then nothing would ever happen to him."

A play on words shortly underscores the point. "He [the whale] says it's time to let go," says Dory. "Everything's gonna be all right." Marlin is still unable to hold on to faith: "How do you know? How do you know something bad isn't gonna happen?" Dory replies, "I don't," and Marlin takes his leap of faith, letting go and falling. It turns out the whale was indeed helping Marlin and Dory, shooting them out of his blow hole right near their destination: Sydney. The play on words is a metaphor for parenting. Sometimes parents have to let go and trust that their children will be all right. We don't know this for sure, of course; something bad might indeed happen, but parents can't carry this burden forever.

An Incredible Family

While *Finding Nemo* is about family, its focus is on one parent and one child—the father, Marlin, and the son, Nemo. *The Incredibles* expands the subject of family and features a unique family, albeit in typical situations and circumstances. The Parr family, aka the Incredibles, consists of a superhero father (Bob) and mother (Helen), and their three children: Violet, Dash and Jack-Jack. They are an extraordinary family in that each of the members possesses superhero abilities. Bob is incredibly strong, Helen can stretch great distances, Violet can become invisible and create force fields,

Dash can move at fantastic speeds, and baby Jack-Jack, at first be-
lieved to have no powers at all, later manifests a variety of them.

Although the Parrs are extraordinary in their super-powered
abilities, they are in many ways ordinary and typical in their expressions related to family. Bob is a father struggling with his job,
doing his best to provide. Helen is a busy mom, juggling household tasks and caring for three children. Violet is a shy teenager
with low self-esteem. Dash is a rambunctious child, testing the
limits of his freedom. Jack-Jack is the baby of the family, adding to
the challenges of daily life. *The Incredibles* admirably handles various family relationships, touching on sibling rivalry, marital
strains and parent-child relationships.

Like *Up*, which we will discuss later, *The Incredibles* brings up a
number of family issues in relation to marriage. When Bob arrives
late to his own wedding due to superhero activities, Helen is direct: "I love you, but if we're gonna make this work, you've gotta
be more than Mr. Incredible. You know that, don't you?" Marriage
is a union, a covenant, a joining, not something to take lightly.
Making it "work," as Helen suggests, takes effort, and part of that
effort involves spending time with family rather than being a
workaholic, being self-centered or being overly preoccupied with
other tasks and interests. Marriage is about two, not one, and thus
offers opportunities for character growth and maturity.

The Incredibles also contains insights into trust in the marriage
relationship. Bob has broken that trust by lying about losing his
job, as well as neglecting to tell Helen about his new superhero
adventures. His apparent midlife crisis is a poor excuse for threatening his marriage relationship or his relationship with his children who, whether he knows it or not, are watching and learning.
When Bob comes home late one evening after supposedly bowling
with his friend, Lucius (aka Frozone), Helen is not pleased. Bob
has obviously been out engaging in superhero activities again.
Helen's concern is having their cover blown again, which would

require a relocation: "Uprooting our family, *again*, so you can re-live the glory days is a very bad thing!" She's also being realistic about their current situation. Yes, Bob had his glory days as Mr. Incredible, but what about now? "This, our family, is what's happening now, Bob! And you are missing this!"

In addition to the marriage relationship, *The Incredibles* also has much to say about parenting. Bob has an unpleasant day at work and comes home bothered, distracted and aloof. His parenting as demonstrated during dinner is limited, unenthusiastic and largely ineffective. When things get out of hand between Violet and Dash, Helen calls out, "Bob, it's time to engage! Do something. Don't just stand there. I need you to intervene!"

Meanwhile, Helen has had quite a day herself, paying a visit to the principal's office because of Dash—his third time sent to the office during that term. "We need to find a better outlet," says Helen, "a more constructive outlet." Dash wants to try out for sports, but his parents haven't allowed him to because they are afraid he won't be able to hide his superhero abilities and will thereby blow their cover. But Dash doesn't understand the restrictions on who he is: "Why can't I do the best I can do?" They just need to fit in, replies Helen—be like everybody else. While the topic of discussion—asking our children to rein in their super abilities!—might not connect to our lives, the discussion itself is illustrative of open and caring parental interaction with children.

Helen's next stop is Western View Junior High, where teenager Violet is waiting for her ride. Violet is shy and awkward, embarrassed by her inability to interact with a boy she likes and lacking in self-esteem. She doesn't say much at the dinner table, appearing bored and withdrawn, and is quick to engage in arguments with the taunting little brother Dash. When Helen uses the phrase "perfectly normal" at one point, Violet exclaims, "Normal? What do you know about normal? What does anyone in this family know about normal?" Although the topic at hand is the possession of superpowers and attempts to blend in despite them, Violet's remarks echo those of many teens about wanting to be normal and wanting to belong.

Later, when Helen approaches the island of Mr. Incredible's nemesis, Syndrome, it turns out that Violet and Dash have stowed away on the jet. During a critical moment, Helen asks Violet to create a force field around the plane, but Violet, under intense pressure, is unable to do so. Not long after, a discussion between Helen and Violet offers additional insights into the parent-child relationship. Violet apologizes for having been unable to generate a force field, but Helen is understanding and reassuring: "It isn't your fault. It wasn't fair for me to suddenly ask so much of you. . . . You have more power than you realize." Helen's tone and inter-action with Violet offer helpful reminders about positive ways we can interact with our children.

About forty minutes into *The Incredibles* is a short montage ac-companied by Michael Giacchino's uplifting score "Life's Incredi-ble Again." The instrumental interlude lasts less than two min-utes, but in that time the film packs in a number of examples of the joys of family life, supported masterfully by the music. Bob truly loves his wife, expressing it with an enthusiastic kiss and playfully chasing Helen around the house. Spending some father-son time with Dash, the two play with race cars and toss a football around. Bob is also more engaged with Jack-Jack. In short, life for Bob and his family is incredible again. Incredible family life doesn't happen on its own, however; it requires active parenting and gen-uine interest.

Families Are Looking Up

A family need not consist of a husband, wife and child. As *Up* demonstrates, a couple, too, constitutes a family. This kind of fam-ily begins with friendship, which grows into love, and in *Up*, leads to marriage. It doesn't matter that Carl and Ellie Fredricksen are in some ways very different. What brings them together as a family is their love. As childhood friends, they share their hopes and dreams, and ultimately they end up marrying, with expectations of going on a grand adventure to South America (see chapters nine and twelve).

In a touching, wordless montage that lasts only a few minutes—accompanied by the beautiful yet wistful music "Married Life," by Giacchino—directors Pete Docter and Bob Peterson show us the story of Carl and Ellie. Carl and Ellie enjoy life and one another, consider having children but are unable to do so, and press on against the challenges of life. Saving money for their trip in a large jar, they still hope to take their adventure to Paradise Falls in South America. Yet life has a way of diminishing our savings because of things like car trouble, home repairs and medical needs. In each case, Carl and Ellie must break open their jar and dip into their adventure funds.

In a flash, many years have gone by, and Carl and Ellie are now elderly. Their dream of visiting Paradise Falls has largely faded from memory. Knowing that their time together is not long, Carl buys tickets to Venezuela and hopes to surprise Ellie while the two are on a picnic. At last they will have their adventure! But it is not to be. Carl's lifelong love, the wife of his youth and old age, dies. Left to himself, Carl loses his perspective on joy and becomes a stereotypical grumpy old man. It takes a unique friendship with a boy named Russell to once again soften Carl's heart (see chapter five).

Telling the story of Carl and Ellie is daring on the part of Pixar. First, the film touches on the painful subject of miscarriage. Second, the wordless montage scene described earlier is a lot for children to absorb. *Up* is about friendship, love, family, and the sacrifices and challenges involved in each. For those who are married, it brings home the reality that at some point one of us will die. What happens to the one who is left behind? But *Up* also highlights the joys of being a family, of being together with the one we love and enjoying what life—what God—has to offer us while we are here. Family can indeed help us grow in virtue.

Unless the Lord Builds the House

"Unless the LORD builds the house, those who build it labor in vain," reads Psalm 127:1. Once again, this verse points out that the key to virtue is found in God alone. A Christian family without Christ at its center will labor in vain. But even without overt references to Christianity, or any religion for that matter, *Finding Nemo* is full of family lessons. Do our children know how much we love them and that we only want what's best for them? Maybe they do, or maybe they don't quite understand the lengths we sometimes go to in order to protect them. Are we around our children enough, or do we spend much of our time elsewhere: at work, with friends or immersed in something that doesn't involve parenting? Like Helen said to Bob, their family is what is important and if he's not careful, he will miss the time they have together. Children need both quality time and a quantity of parental time, not just quick interludes of attention.

It may be cliché, but children grow up fast. Do we want to look back on the time we spent with our children only to say to ourselves, *I wish we'd had more time together?* Children grow up and leave, so we should make the most of our time with them, helping them on their way to becoming the kind of people God would want them to be, helping them grow in character so that they can make a positive difference in the lives of others and in the world.

In the end, the Parrs lose nearly everything of material value, including their home and the new cars Bob purchased. In the process of losing everything, however, they gain something more important: the unique closeness and love that only a family can provide. Marlin learns many lessons about being a parent, while Nemo grows in confidence and learns the depths of Marlin's love for him. Carl loses Ellie, the love of his life, but in the end he is grateful for the adventure of their joyous time together. No matter how ordinary it may seem, love is always extraordinary. And so is family.

Discussion Questions

1. What elements of family can you relate to best: those found in *Finding Nemo, The Incredibles* or *Up?* Why?

2. If you are a parent, where do you fit on the spectrum of being overprotective or overly lenient? Are you more like Marlin or Crush? Is there an ideal balance between the two parenting approaches?

3. The daily pressures of getting through life can take their toll on any family. Given the biblical view of the family with God as the foundation, how should Christian families approach challenges and trials?

4. The Bible presents God as Father and Christians as God's children. What are your impressions of the terms *father* and *child* in reference to your relationship with God?

COURAGE

The Incredibles—
"Where's my Super suit?"

Lucius Best is preparing for a romantic dinner date with his wife. Soft jazz music plays in the background while he puts on his cologne. The mood is shattered when Lucius hears noises coming from outside. He looks out the windows of his classy high-rise apartment in Metroville (think New York) and sees a giant robot being chased by a helicopter. So much for a quiet evening. Lucius doesn't hesitate, grabbing a remote control that triggers secret compartments to open in the walls.

Lucius is not what he seems. He is Frozone, a superhero capable of utilizing moisture in the air to make ice and freeze objects. But something's wrong; his Super suit is missing! "Honey," he calls to his wife, "where's my Super suit?" He dashes through his apartment, anxious to find his superhero attire and enter the battle against the destructive robot known as the Omnidroid. His wife is not pleased: "Don't you think about runnin' out and doin' no derrin'-do. We've been planning this dinner for two months!" Frozone is unwavering: "The public is in danger!" His wife doesn't budge, adding, "My evening's in danger!"

Frozone doesn't stop to ponder the ethical questions surrounding the virtue of courage. Nor does he pull a textbook on ethics off the shelf in order to consult what it says about courage. He just reacts, knowing that he must do the morally right thing. But

ACTION!

The Incredibles
U.S. Release Date: November 5, 2004

Director Brad Bird's original story for *The Incredibles* featured a character named Xerek as the primary villain, with Syndrome playing a secondary role. Contrary to popular belief among some graphic novel fans, *The Incredibles* was not inspired by *Watchmen*, which also tells the story of superheroes forced into hiding, albeit in much grittier surroundings.

how did he get this way? Is it mere instinct, ingrained in him by years of superhero service? Or is there more to his courage?

What about us? We're not superheroes. Is courage only for those who are extraordinary in some way, or is it an everyday virtue that we, too, can exhibit? The chances that we will need to battle giant robots are, shall we say, slim! But that does not exclude us from seeking to understand and live out the virtue of courage.

The Roots of Courage

One of the four cardinal virtues, courage (fortitude) was valued by the ancient Greeks along with justice, prudence (wisdom) and temperance. Unlike cowardice that gives in to fear, courage overcomes fear in order to do what is morally right. Granting the reality of natural law—that God has instilled in us a moral compass—the virtue of courage is, at some level, ingrained in everyone. Acts of heroism and altruism—that is, selfless and possibly dangerous actions that foster the well-being of others—occur because of the reality of this virtue. Darwinian natural selection, with its emphasis on survival of the fittest, does not adequately explain such acts. True courage, in fact, often goes against the underlying principles of natural selection. Instead of emphasizing self-preservation, the courageous take risks in order to help others, with nothing to be gained for the hero other than moral character growth. A world without courage is a world driven by fear and selfishness.

Unfortunately, like any virtue, courage can be warped into a vice. For instance, if a criminal develops courage to continue committing crimes, the purity of courage is defaced. We may say that the criminal in question has become bold or daring, but this is not the same as courage as a virtue. By its very nature, virtue seeks the good, not the bad.

Biblically speaking, courage is established in God and his nature. It's not just about controlling our fears on our own steam, so to speak. Rather, having confidence in God and his attributes should form the foundation of Christian courage. We should be courageous not for the wrong reasons, such as pride in order to gain attention for ourselves, but because we trust in God. Identity also plays into the Christian view of courage. Knowing who we are in Christ is important in developing any Christian virtue.

Understanding a virtue is usually quite simple; living it out on a consistent, day-to-day basis is often difficult. We can't expect to read an article about courage, or even a chapter in a book, and suddenly know everything we need to know about being courageous. When it comes to cultivating foundational virtues, growth and development in our spiritual life will take time. Unfortunately, we won't always succeed. Sometimes we will, frankly, act less than virtuously. The goal is not perfection in this life but practice in our daily lives; over time, such practice will help us make the right moral choices when we have the opportunity.

Pixar's Courage

So what can Pixar films teach us about courage? Plenty. In *Toy Story*, Woody comes up with a courageous plan to rescue Buzz from the destructive machinations of the troubled neighbor boy, Sid, who enjoys torturing toys. In *Toy Story 2*, Woody risks his own life to bravely save the life of the penguin, Wheezy, who has been placed in the twenty-five-cent bin of a yard sale. In *Monsters, Inc.*, one monster helps another build up courage by telling him, "Keep it together, man!" WALL-E the mischievous robot may not comprehend exactly what he is doing, but his behavior is illustrative of courage when he pursues the robot EVE by desperately clinging to a spaceship that is about to launch. We may question the methods of Carl Fredricksen in *Up*, but his desire to fulfill his wife's wishes is indeed courageous.

Examples of courage taken from *The Incredibles*, *A Bug's Life* and *Cars* will suffice for our purposes.

Incredible Courage

Since it revolves around superheroes, or "Supers" as the film calls them, *The Incredibles* is filled with expressions of courage and heroism. From the opening sequence featuring Bob Parr (Mr. Incredible) in his prime—chasing gun-wielding criminals, rescuing a man who has jumped off a building, stopping a train headed for a nasty fall, even rescuing Whiskers the cat—the action is riveting. Later Mr. Incredible teams up with Frozone to rescue people from a burning building, defeat an Omnidroid prototype and relentlessly pursue the truth behind the villain Syndrome's nefarious plans.

But Bob is not the only Super expressing courage. His wife, Helen, used to be Elastigirl, a Super with the ability to stretch her body great distances like elastic. When she suspects her marriage is in danger, as well as Bob's life, she takes the courageous action of finding him, arriving on Syndrome's island (cleverly named Nomanisan Island). After seeing that her stowaway children are safe, Elastigirl proceeds to investigate Syndrome's compound, where she finds and rescues Mr. Incredible; together, they join up with their children and continue the battle against Syndrome and eventually team up in Metroville to defeat the seemingly unstoppable Omnidroid.

But it's not these overt acts of courage, these larger-than-life heroics, that most of us who are mere mortals can relate to. It makes for plenty of action and entertainment, but the virtue of courage does not penetrate us too deeply in these scenes. Instead, it is the everyday courage that *The Incredibles* demonstrates on a practical level that draws our interest.

A former Super longing for the glory days of his prime, Mr. Incredible is forced into hiding as a result of the government-initiated Superhero Relocation Program. Fifteen years later and facing something of a midlife crisis, Bob is stuck in a dead-end job. He is unhappy and unfulfilled, but he keeps at it, day after day, not for his sake, but for that of his wife and three children who rely on his support.

We may not think of Bob's behavior as courageous, but it is. Certainly it's not a flashy sort of courage like what he was used to as Mr. Incredible, but it shows fortitude—a willingness to endure adversity for a greater purpose, in this case his family. Near the end of the film, Bob has learned some powerful lessons about his identity and his family. As the Parrs hang helpless in Syndrome's contraption built to restrain Supers by using powerful energy streams, Bob begins his apology, blaming himself for having been a "lousy father . . . so obsessed with being undervalued that I undervalued all of you." It's easy to point out the shortcomings of others, but it takes courage to fess up to our own.

Bugged by Courage

We've already addressed the theme of justice in *A Bug's Life*, but pursuing justice almost always requires courage. To make right what is wrong isn't always easy or pleasant. The point of acting virtuously, however, is not to make us feel good or make our lives easier. In reality, doing the right thing is often difficult. As *A Bug's Life* demonstrates, courage may manifest itself both individually and collectively.

Individually, courage is best represented by Flik, a simple, creative, bungling ant who sincerely wants what's best for his colony. But it will take time for his courage and confidence to grow. The first example of Flik's courage comes not long after the angry grasshoppers arrive only to find their food offering missing. As the ant colony cowers, the grasshoppers, who are used to getting their way and who are intent on spreading fear, break into their hole. The oppressors do what they do best—intimidate the small and weak. Hopper, their leader, places his four hands behind his back and struts around, gazing at the frightened ants. "So where is it?" he asks menacingly, referring to the expected food offering. When Hopper snatches up the little Princess Dot, no one does anything—they are too terrified. Only one ant has the courage to say something. Flik steps out from beyond the crowd and calls out to Hopper, "Leave her alone!" Flik's courage is short-lived, as the bullying Hopper frightens Flik back into submission. Still, the tendency toward courage is within Flik—"bugging" him, we might say—as it is within each of us. It will take a later event in the film for Flik's courage to grow and, in turn, make a real difference.

Flik's plan to save the colony literally goes down in flames when a fake bird is set on fire by P. T. Flea. Hopper once again bullies Flik, but this time a simple talking-to isn't enough. Using the muscle of his crazed hench-grasshopper Thumper, Hopper has Flik beaten. Although the heroic ant is weak and injured, Flik has the courage to contradict Hopper, who is busy humiliating the ants. "Ants are not meant to serve grasshoppers," says Flik. He goes on, standing up to Hopper as the rest of the ant colony looks on in awe.

Flik's individual courage soon grows into collective courage as the colony begins to murmur, pondering Flik's words. As Hopper is about to crush Flik's head, Princess Atta demonstrates her share of courage when she steps in front of Hopper. The entire colony is now angry, resolved to fight the grasshoppers if need be. It is now the grasshoppers who are on the defensive, greatly outnumbered by the ants. The battle for ant justice begins and, fortunately, succeeds.

Fueling Our Courage

In *Cars*, Pixar offers yet another take on courage. Lightning Mc-Queen isn't particularly courageous, but at the end of *Cars* he has certainly grown in character. Once a cocky race car with nothing else on his mind but winning the tie-breaking Piston Cup race, Lightning now has other things to think about, such as his friends and what he has learned from them about doing the right thing (see chapter nine). In the final lap, Dinoco's retiring star Strip "The King" Weathers is in the lead, and the win-at-all-costs Chick Hicks is trailing in second place. (Chick's sponsor, incidentally, reveals a lot about his general attitude toward racing: htB, for "hostile takeover Bank.") Lightning McQueen is in third, but coming up fast he soon takes the lead, leaving The King in second and Hicks in third.

Chick is not happy. Racing in the shadow of Strip Weathers is not something he wants to do. "I am not comin' in behind you again, old man," growls Hicks, who has trailed behind Weathers far too often. Playing dirty once again, Hicks smashes into The King, sending him rolling over and over until Strip comes to a stop, battered and out of the race. Meanwhile, Lightning has taken a comfortable lead. His victory in the Piston Cup is assured. Winning, after all, is what he has wanted more than anything. But he becomes concerned when he sees the image of the battered Strip Weathers on a large television screen. Lightning is reminded of the photograph of Doc Hudson, aka the Hudson Hornet, in an old newspaper, similarly battered, defeated and ultimately forgotten. Although Lightning has only recently met Doc, he knows about the pain Hudson went through years ago as a result of a serious crash during a race.

Seconds away from the checkered flag and his first Piston Cup win, Lightning makes a courageous decision. He stops, just feet from the finish line. Hicks passes him and wins the race. Lightning drives over to Strip. "I think The King should finish his last race," says Lightning, as he begins to push The King toward the finish line. Doesn't Lightning want to win? He has just given up the Piston Cup, as Weathers points out. "It's just an empty cup," says Lightning, echoing the words of Doc Hudson, who now understands all too well the difference between having trophies and having friends.

Meanwhile, Hicks is busy doing donuts on the grass, celebrating his win, but nobody cares (later he is booed off stage). Everyone watches as Lightning pushes The King into second place, while McQueen comes in third (and last). Tremendous applause fills the stadium. Why? Because one car had the courage to do something extraordinary, not for himself, but for someone else in need. Lightning did not win the race, but, ironically, by losing he has indeed won. Lightning has grown in other ways, too, not just in courage. When he's offered the prestigious Dinoco sponsorship, Lightning turns it down, deciding to stick with Rust-eze, grateful to them for giving him his first opportunity to race. As he approaches his friends, the gravelly voice of Doc Hudson, voiced by the inimitable Paul Newman, remarks, "You got a lot of stuff, kid." Indeed he does, including the stuff of courage.

Be Strong and Courageous

God calls us to "be strong and courageous" (Deuteronomy 31:6-7, 23; Joshua 1:6-7, 9, 18). But how? We can't just flip a virtue switch on our backs, select the best moral trait suited to our situation and suddenly become courageous. Rather, making the right ethical decisions is the result of many factors, not the least of which is our

firm foundation in Christ and our desire to serve him honorably.
We also need to practice virtue regularly, not neglecting the difference it will make to the whole of our character, as even small
choices will contribute to our overall nature (for better or for
worse). How do we "practice" virtue? By making a conscious effort
to make the best ethical choices every day that we are faced with
such decisions.

Unless we have a job in which opportunities for overt heroism
and courage are available on a regular basis—such as a police officer, firefighter or soldier—many of us may never find ourselves
in a situation in which we can display that kind of courage. We
certainly will not be in a position to defeat an Omnidroid, stop a
train headed for disaster with only our brute strength or stand up
in defense of an oppressed ant colony. This does not mean, however, that in our daily lives we will not encounter situations that
require courage. Maybe we will be tempted to tell a lie rather than
the truth, or to make a wrong but popular decision that will avoid
scorn or ridicule. Most important of all, we need to remember the
ultimate foundation of our courage is confidence in God, not ourselves or others.

It's easier to be a coward—to run away from responsibility, to
hide from danger, to refuse to own up to our shortcomings and
flaws. But cowardice in such situations is not the right thing to do;
courage is. Lightning McQueen had a choice to make. He could
have gone on to win the Piston Cup, but in a matter of seconds he
made the courageous decision to go back and help the battered
Strip Weathers. Morally right choices are not often easy to make.
In fact, they are usually difficult, because they challenge us. But if
this world is, in part, a moral training ground for us, preparing us
for eternity, then we need to do our best to learn what we can
about the virtues God desires to grow in us. We need to make the
moral choices that are not necessarily expedient but right.

By its very nature, individual courage places us outside the crowd. It's not always popular to go against the many, to stand out, to say and do things that are uncommon. But the heroes of history are remembered for just these kinds of acts. Moral reformers stand out from the crowd, whether it is William Wilberforce opposing slavery, Mahatma Gandhi exercising civil disobedience for the sake of civil rights, Mother Teresa ministering to those in need or countless other courageous heroes. Ideas, too, can be courageous, and can set us up against the status quo.

One final note about Lightning McQueen's loss of the Piston Cup is in order. The world tends to have a skewed definition of winning, but Christ's perspective is quite radical: "For whoever would save his life will lose it, but whoever loses his life for my sake and the gospel's will save it. For what does it profit a man to gain the whole world and forfeit his soul?" (Mark 8:35-36). If we lose everything, yet have gained Christ, in truth that is all we need to win.

Discussion Questions

1. Lucius Best is preparing for a quiet evening with his wife when his comfortable plans are suddenly interrupted. Sometimes our plans are interrupted as well, but are "interruptions" in our lives really interruptions? Maybe God has other plans for us via what we consider interruptions. The next time you are interrupted, take a moment to consider what God may want to teach you and how you might act virtuously in the situation. What might you do to better prepare yourself for God's "interruptions"?

2. The Bible calls us to "be strong and courageous." What is the foundation of our courage? How so?

3. Lightning McQueen gave up the Piston Cup in order to courageously do the right thing. When faced with difficult situations,

what can you do in order to better live out Christ's words in Mark 8:35: "For whoever would save his life will lose it, but whoever loses his life for my sake and the gospel's will save it"? How would you explain that verse and parallel passages? See Matthew 16:25; Luke 9:24; and John 12:25.

4. Think of a moral reformer you admire. Why do you admire this person? What moral attributes in this person could you seek to emulate?

ADVENTURE

Cars—
"Life is a journey."

Do we plan adventure, or does it simply happen in unexpected ways? Lightning McQueen is a successful Piston Cup race car, an ambitious rookie intent on one thing alone: winning. His adventure is planned. He will race and win, become the best, and upgrade his sponsor from the embarrassing Rust-eze medicated bumper ointment company to the prestigious Dinoco. Life will be perfect—or so he thinks. While being transported to California for a tie-breaking race, Lightning is accidentally left behind en route. Alone on a busy interstate, McQueen panics, becomes disoriented, foolishly outruns a train and winds up on Route 66. A misunderstanding results in Lightning fleeing from a police car and into the forgotten, quiet town of Radiator Springs, where he causes extensive damage when he inadvertently drags the statue of the city's founder, Stanley, down the main street, ruining the road.

The town's residents live at a slow, thoughtful pace—nothing at all like what Lightning is used to on the Piston Cup circuit. His

ACTION!

Cars

U.S. Release Date: June 9, 2006

In just a few years, *Cars* has made more than $5 billion in merchandising sales alone. This is an astounding number considering that the *Star Wars* franchise, consisting of six live-action feature films that began in 1977, has made an estimated $9 billion in product sales over the course of more than thirty years. Given these numbers, it's no wonder that a sequel, *Cars 2,* is set for a 2011 release.

plans of reaching California early in order to woo Dinoco to become his sponsor are dashed when he finds himself in an impound lot, then sentenced to repairing the damage he has done to Radiator Springs. Lightning is not pleased. He does not initially see his unexpected adventure as an adventure at all, but as a nuisance—a costly delay to his career plans. He is bitter, angry, sarcastic and, in general, unfriendly. Though somewhat formulaic with its fish-out-of-water storyline and some parallels reminiscent of *Doc Hollywood* (1991), *Cars* brings to life the spirit of adventure communicated in one of the taglines for the film: "Life is a journey. Enjoy the trip."

Lightning ends up learning a lot from his accidental exile. His detour into Radiator Springs ultimately teaches him about identity, friendship, courage, misplaced ambitions and, of course, adventure. Life is indeed a journey, but it is one that too many of us fail to appreciate due to our own misplaced ideas and ideals. Maybe we are caught up in the day-to-day challenges of life, are overly focused on our jobs, or are too busy to slow down and "enjoy the trip" that God has in store for us. Whatever the case may be, understanding adventure will help us better understand life.

Unusual Adventures

We can probably think of times in our lives in which we've experienced what we'd call an adventure. Maybe it involved taking a trip, exploring part of the country unknown to us, or doing something a bit risky yet strangely enjoyable. *Adventure*, by definition, is unusual. It's not generally seen as the same old thing we're used to doing, day after day. At some level, adventure involves risk, and risk exposes us to uncertainty. Despite the varying degrees of danger posed by adventure, most of us view the positive aspects of adventure as worth the risk.

Adventures abound in the Bible. Most take place within the context of obedience to God despite human reservations and uncertainty. When Moses encounters a burning bush and hears the voice of God, he hesitates and even makes excuses for why he's not the best choice for God's plans. Yet ahead of Moses is a grand adventure that will ultimately lead his people out of slavery (see Exodus 3 and following). It's not all about fun and excitement, though. There are obstacles, challenges, setbacks and disappointments. The faith of Moses wavers, as does the faith of the Israelites at times. God calls each of us to a life full of adventure, but not necessarily to the sort of adventure we expect. In fact, it's usually the sort of adventure we *don't* have in mind that, ironically, happens to us.

Adventure is not just about going out into the world. We may take an intellectual adventure, or we may have an inner decision-making struggle that leads to adventure. Or we may have a seemingly ordinary life that is, in reality, an extraordinary adventure if only we'd take a moment to step back and look at it more carefully. In *The Incredibles*, when Mr. Incredible and his family are being held captive by Syndrome, Bob is remorseful. Admitting to his recent shortcomings as a husband and father, his words are full of meaning: "You are my greatest adventure, and I almost missed it." Life with family is an adventure, but we don't always see it as such.

How is adventure like a virtue? It's not usually thought of as being particularly virtuous. Adventure need not demonstrate particularly high moral values at all. Some adventures may, in fact, be contrary to virtue. Biblically speaking, adventure is like a virtue when we find ourselves trusting God and doing what we were called to do. When we do so, life is indeed a journey and we can enjoy the trip.

Pixar's Adventures

What's a movie without adventure? Probably not a very good movie. Fortunately, Pixar's films are full of adventure. *Toy Story* finds Buzz and Woody lost and on an adventure at Pizza Planet and, later, at Sid's house. In *A Bug's Life*, Flik, who tries not to look like a country bug, goes on a quest to find warriors to help his colony. *Toy Story 2* opens with a spectacular Buzz Lightyear adventure to defeat the evil Zurg, which turns out to just be a video game sequence. But that doesn't stop the toys from having other adventures involving rescuing Woody from Al McWhiggin the toy collector and rescuing Jessie from the cargo hold of a plane bound for Japan. *Monsters, Inc.* finds Sulley and Mike on an adventure to help the human child, Boo. They risk their jobs in the process and also expose the fiendish plans of Waternoose and Randall, who plan to extract screams from children by force. *The Incredibles*, *Ratatouille*, *WALL-E* and other Pixar films have their share of adventure too. For our purposes, let's explore the themes of adventure in *Up* and *Finding Nemo*.

Adventure Is Out There!

The Pixar film with the most overt references to adventure is undoubtedly *Up*. The opening newsreel sequence is all about Charles Muntz, an explorer who travels the world in his enormous dirigible airship dubbed *Spirit of Adventure*. "Adventure is out there!" proclaims Muntz enthusiastically. His larger-than-life persona and adventures inspire a generation of children, including young Carl Fredricksen and his future wife, Ellie, who forms her own club and exclaims, "Only explorers get in here!" Ellie later shares her adventure book with a duly impressed Carl. *My Adventure*

Book, as it is titled, is full of "stuff I'm going to do," and plays a key role in Carl's decision to go on an adventure many years later after Ellie has passed away.

It's clear that Carl misses Ellie. Their life together did not take them to South America, as they had dreamed, but it nevertheless gave them love and joy. Now an elderly and curmudgeonly man, Carl has in many ways lost hope, along with losing his wife. Skyscrapers are going up around the quaint little home he shared with Ellie for so many years, while legal actions are threatening to move him to the Shady Oaks Retirement Home. Carl flips through Ellie's adventure book and sees a drawing of their home right next to Paradise Falls.

Intent on fulfilling Ellie's wishes, Carl embarks on the adventure of his life. He attaches so many balloons to his house that it lifts off and takes him on a journey to South America. Interestingly, Carl's adventure is for Ellie, not for himself. But on the way he ends up having his own adventure too. When Carl finally makes it to Paradise Falls, landing his home on the spot in Ellie's drawing, he sits down to look at her adventure book once more. He finds some pages he hadn't seen before—pages that focus on Ellie's life with him—and at the end sees a note: "Thanks for the adventure—now go have a new one!" Carl finally understands that even though Ellie never traveled to South America or visited Paradise Falls or met her hero Charles Muntz, she still had an adventure: life with him. It was not the kind of adventure that Carl expected.

What matters most is not necessarily going on a dangerous journey to exotic places. Sometimes our greatest adventures are right in front of us, if we'll only stop to look. The life God has called us to may be filled with adventure even though we don't see it as such. We need to open our eyes to what might be termed *ordinary adventures*—the daily challenges we face and overcome, our jobs, church involvement, time with family and countless other seemingly ordinary events.

Adventures in Parenting

How is Homer's *Odyssey* like *Finding Nemo*? They're not identical, but there are some similarities. Odysseus, also known as Ulysses, spends years after the Trojan War on a journey that will reunite him with his family. Marlin is also on an adventure—an odyssey—that will reunite him with his missing son, Nemo. What drives Marlin's adventure is not his adventurous spirit. Truth be told, he has the opposite of an adventurous spirit, preferring the safety and familiarity of his quiet anemone home to the dangers of the outside world. As the hobbit Bilbo Baggins used to say to his nephew, Frodo, "It's a dangerous business going out your front door. . . . You step into the Road, and if you don't keep your feet, there is no knowing where you might be swept off to."[1]

Like Carl, however, Marlin is not driven by a desire to have an adventure. Rather, his adventure comes about unexpectedly, unfolding as part of his quest to find Nemo. Also like *Up*, the adventure in *Finding Nemo* is spurred by love, unfolding in ways Marlin never would have dreamed and, in the process, helping him become a better parent. Any parent will tell you that parenting is an adventure. In its day-to-day manifestations, parenting doesn't usually involve trips to South America, encounters with hungry sharks or hot-air balloon rides, but that doesn't make it any less of an adventure in its own right. Parenting is a joy, a challenge, a burden and also a delight. Marlin's undersea adventure helps us see that from a different perspective.

At the beginning of *Finding Nemo*, Marlin is paranoid about Nemo's first day of school, exhibiting his typical overprotectiveness. By the end of the film, Marlin has learned some important lessons. His adventure has introduced him to many creatures and he has learned from each of them. From his friend Dory, he learns to have faith. From Crush the sea turtle, Marlin learns that sometimes it's best to let children have an adventure and to overcome challenges on their own. He also learns to have fun while on an adventure, rather than seeing everything negatively and as a potential danger. When escaping from jellyfish, Marlin proclaims, "So, we're cheating death now, that's what we're doing. We're having fun at the same time. I can do this, just be careful." With Nemo finally safe and back home, Marlin displays the new attitude that he learned while on his adventures. Rather than fretting over Nemo as he goes off to school, Marlin now says to his son, "Now go have an adventure!" The clownfish father is still a caring parent, but Marlin now lets his son learn and grow as an individual.

Enjoying the Trip

John Lasseter, chief creative officer at Pixar, has said that the story behind the film *Cars* was inspired by his own life. Lasseter had worked long hours on *Toy Story, Toy Story 2* and *A Bug's Life* when his wife, Nancy, reminded him of the importance of spending time with his five boys: "Be careful. One day you're going to wake up and the boys will have gone off to college, and you will have missed it." Upon completion of *Toy Story 2*, Lasseter took the summer off and went on a two-month cross-country RV road trip with his family. As Lasseter recalled, "I reconnected with my family in a way I hadn't been able to do for a long time. Being on the road together with them, having this great adventure driving the small highways and going where the wind blew us, made me realize that the journey truly is the reward."[2]

Adventure can be found in the most unexpected places. Maybe we're moving to a new place, getting a different job, graduating from high school or college, anticipating marriage, or expecting our first child or grandchild. All of these experiences are filled with an everyday adventure that we often miss or fail to acknowledge as an adventure. Is there a Paradise Falls that we long to journey to, thinking that only then we will be on a *real* adventure? Maybe we will get to our Paradise Falls; maybe we won't. In either case, adventure is out there for us, often closer than we think.

Near the end of *Toy Story 2*, Buzz asks Woody if he's still worried about Andy growing up and discarding his toys. "Nah," says Woody. "It'll be fun while it lasts. Besides, when it all ends, I'll have old Buzz Lightyear to keep me company, for infinity and beyond." Woody has learned to enjoy the journey, not obsess about what might happen along the way.

Christianity is an adventure, although we probably don't always think of it as such. It is, of course, a spiritual journey, and it may not take us to some distant and exotic land (although it might). But there is much about being a Christian that has affinities with the concept of adventure. In Acts 9:2 we learn that Christianity was also known as "the Way." Derived from the Greek word *hodos*, "the Way" literally referred to a road or path—a way of getting from point A to point B. In broader terms, Christianity as "the Way" is about the Christian life as a whole.

What keeps us from having the adventure God intends for us? We do. We don't want to take the risk that is before us, we don't trust God, or we are uncertain or perhaps embarrassed by following the path God has placed before us. In short, it's a matter of faith. If we do indeed trust God at a foundational level, then the adventure God has for us is something we should embrace. Not embracing God's adventure, however, does not make us failures; it only means we're human. As we have seen, even biblical heroes such as Moses struggled with God's adventure. The key, then, is overcoming our fears and reservations on the basis of God's unwavering nature, attributes and promises. This is often easier said than done. One approach to growing to trust God is to follow Christ's advice in Matthew 6:33: "But seek first the kingdom of God and his righteousness."

Discussion Questions

1. Can you think of at least one thing that is keeping you from

enjoying God's adventure for your life? What steps could you take to overcome the obstacle?

2. Adventures are often unexpected, as was the case for Lightning McQueen in *Cars*. Are there areas in your life where you are moving so fast that you might not enjoy the journey? What can you do to slow down in those areas?

3. John Lasseter took a road trip with his family and realized that "the journey truly is the reward." How can you better enjoy the adventure with your family?

4. What is your Paradise Falls? That is, what is it that you see as your grand adventure in life? How will you get there? Do you think it is part of God's adventure for you?

5. Think of something seemingly ordinary that you will do this week. How can you approach it as something with the potential for adventure? How might you change your attitude in order to look for adventure in unexpected places?

10

AMBITION

Ratatouille—
"I want to make things."

Alfredo Linguini has had it rough. An orphan who can't seem to hold down a steady job, Linguini sheepishly approaches Gusteau's restaurant in Paris, hoping to find work. He's offered a position as garbage boy and quickly accepts it. But things in Linguini's world are quickly thrown out of balance when a rat shows up in the kitchen. This is no ordinary rat, however. It is an extraordinary rat named Remy, who possesses a great love for delicious food as well as a desire to cook. Remy succeeds in making a delicious soup out of the food ruined by Linguini, who had been adding various ingredients when no one else was looking. While Skinner, the head chef, is berating Linguini, everyone springs into action when they see a rat. The timid, red-haired Linguini catches Remy in a jar and asks the chef, "What should I do now?" Skinner doesn't miss a beat: "Kill it! . . . Take it away from here. Kill it, dispose of it! Go!"

Linguini finds himself on his bicycle roaming the streets of

Paris at night. His mission is to destroy the rat. Stopping by the river Seine, Linguini sadly carries the jar to the edge of the river and looks into the running water below. Remy is shocked, breathing rapidly and eyes bulging. "Don't look at me like that!" says Linguini. "You aren't the only one who's trapped. They expect me to cook it again," utters Linguini, referring to the soup made by Remy that turned out to be a hit. "I mean," adds Linguini, "I'm not ambitious; I wasn't trying to cook. I was just trying to stay out of trouble." He grabs the jar with both hands and looks menacingly at the incarcerated rat: "You're the one who was getting fancy with the spices!"

ACTION!

Ratatouille

U.S. Release Date: June 29, 2007

Critics and audiences alike were somewhat skeptical of a Pixar film featuring a rat who enjoys cooking. This may account for the fact that *Ratatouille* had the second lowest opening weekend for a Pixar movie since *A Bug's Life* (1998). Ultimately, however, *Ratatouille* went on to earn more than $624 million globally, making it the fourth top-grossing Pixar film to date, trailing *Finding Nemo* ($866 million), *Up* ($711 million) and *The Incredibles* ($635 million). Nominated for five Academy Awards, *Ratatouille* won Best Animated Feature Film, proving that a properly animated rodent, combined with a successful story, can indeed win the rat race.

Moreover, Remy, unlike Linguini, *is* ambitious. He admires human beings and their creativity (see chapter two). Not content with being a typical rat, merely surviving and stealing food, Remy wants more out of life. As Remy later explains to his skeptical father, Django, "Rats! All we do is take, Dad. I'm tired of taking. I want to make things. I want to add something to this world." And therein lies Remy's ambition. He desires to make a positive difference in the world and not just to take but to give. When Linguini and Remy join forces, Remy is able to pursue his ambition and cook the best food he can.

But is ambition related to virtue? If so, how? It's one thing for a computer-animated rat to ambitiously pursue his dreams and aspirations, but what about in the real world? Is there a place for ambition in the Christian life?

Ambition: Positive and Negative

In a general sense, ambition is simply a powerful desire to do something and, as such, is related to achievement and success. Ambition and hard work are often associated, since ambition usually means striving for something that is not easy to achieve. Aspiration is tied to ambition, too, insofar as aspiration means hoping to achieve some distinction by reaching a goal.

In the Bible, ambition is often connected to vice. Ambition resulted in the pride of Satan, for instance, that caused his downfall, and the ambitions of Adam and Eve in the Genesis account led to the Fall. Ambition is also said to lead to vanity and strife. When the disciples asked Jesus, "Who is the greatest in the kingdom of heaven?" (Matthew 18:1), a case could be made that his response applies not only to pride but to ambition. Jesus replied, "Truly, I say to you, unless you turn and become like children, you will never enter the kingdom of heaven. Whoever humbles himself like this child is the greatest in the kingdom of heaven" (Matthew 18:3-4). Little children are not known for caring about their social status or having grand and worldly ambitions. They thus exemplify humility, even though they are not actively seeking to be humble.

If ambition is not generally seen as a virtue but as a vice, why, then, does a book about wisdom and virtue include a chapter on ambition? Although ambition can indeed lead to vice, properly pursued it can also be virtuous. In Romans 15:20, for instance, Paul says, "Thus I make it my ambition to preach the gospel," providing an exception to the perception that ambition is always bad. In other words, we must guard against negative ambition, such as the "selfish ambition" described in James 3:14 and 16. Instead, we can cultivate positive ambition that is beneficial.

Looking at the Greek underlying English translations of the New Testament, we find there are actually two primary words translated as "ambition": *eritheia* and *philotimeomai*. The former, *eritheia*, has negative connotations, such as in James 3:14 and 16, where it is translated as "selfish ambition," and in Romans 2:8, where it is translated as "self-seeking." Obviously this is the negative sort of ambition that is self-centered rather than God-centered.

The other word, however, *philotimeomai*, may be translated "godly ambition." Its goal is the good. Rather than being self-centered, this kind of ambition seeks to please God, such as in 2 Corinthians 5:9, where it is often translated as "goal" or "aim," with the goal being to please God. The emphasis of this kind of ambition, then, is on others and on God, rather than on the self or on one's own pride. The differences between these two words are important. As we mature in Christ and in the virtues he desires to cultivate in us, our focus shifts to God and others and away from ourselves. This does not mean that we completely neglect ourselves and our own spiritual and physical needs; it does mean, however, that as godly virtue matures in us, we are more often than not concerned about others due to our love for God.

This is not to say that there are only two kinds of ambition: God-centered and self-centered. Someone may, for instance, eagerly and ambitiously pursue something not for herself or himself or God but for her or his family. This, too, is a positive, altruistic form of ambition that seeks to help others. Granted, the person may not even consider God at this juncture; yet a positive expression of virtue of any kind is desirable, and may perhaps even prepare a person for future godly virtues.

Pixar's Ambitions

What about Pixar and ambition? We've already mentioned *Ratatouille* and will return to it shortly. Other Pixar films also feature ambitious characters of one kind or another. In *A Bug's Life*, Flik has ambitions as an inventor. He desires to improve the quality of life for ants in his colony, although he hasn't had much success. "I'm never gonna make a difference," he says dejectedly. Underlying his external disappointment, however, is his desire to make a positive difference, and this desire is ambition. This also moves Flik to leave his colony in search of help against the bullying grasshoppers. In short, ambition drives Flik to become what we might term a moral reformer seeking justice (see chapter four).

Monsters, Inc., on the other hand, features a character with warped ambitions. Randall is a purple, eight-legged, lizard-like creature who desires to beat coworker Sulley as the top "scarer." Randall is also ambitious in his desire to use a machine called a "scream extractor" to harness the power of children's screams and thus to rise to the top of Monsters, Incorporated. He is ambitious in the self-centered sense. He also wants to have others be subservient to him, going so far as to express his desire to have "the great James P. Sullivan" (Sulley) working under him after Randall revolutionizes the scare industry.

Lightning McQueen also has his share of ambition in *Cars*, with his goal being to win races. His ambition is not nearly as warped as that of Randall or of fellow Piston Cup racer Chick Hicks, who goes so far as to deliberately cause accidents so that he can win races. Nevertheless, Lightning's ambition is indeed self-centered.

Cultured Rat

What sets *Ratatouille* apart is that it offers an excellent example of ambition in relation to culture. Too often Christians fail to make positive and lasting contributions to culture, in part because they lack understanding of their role in relation to culture. As Andy Crouch has written, "*Culture is what we make of the world. Culture is, first of all, the name for our relentless, restless human effort to take the world as it's given to us and make something else. This is the original insight of the writer of Genesis when he says that hu-*

man beings were made in God's image: just like the original Creator, we are creators."[1]

Of course, *Ratatouille* doesn't set out to offer itself as a role model specifically for Christian viewers eager to make a difference in culture; it does, however, offer many insights into the creative imagination in relation to cultural betterment. Remy desires to "make things" and "to add something to this world" rather than merely going with the flow and "taking." Remy's specific use of "taking" is interesting in that it can relate to what most of us are in culture: consumers. However, we should also seek to be producers—creating and contributing positively to our culture.

Note, too, that Remy's ambition to make things and add something of value to the world is inspired by his perception of humans. As we touched on in chapter two, Remy admires the creativity in humans, noting, "They don't just survive, they discover, they create!" Having been made in God's image, we have identities that involve creativity, which is tied to ambition. Chef Auguste Gusteau, moreover, rightly compares the preparation of good food to an artistic endeavor. Historically, Christians have made significant contributions to the arts not because of selfish ambition, but because of God-honoring ambition that takes seriously the mandate to be salt and light in the world and to express God-given creativity in every area of life. Creative passions are, unfortunately, far too often suppressed or misunderstood within contemporary Western expressions of Christianity.

Influencing culture positively should not be seen in negative terms as a chore or burden, but as a delight. Remy delights in cooking, expressing joy in the process rather than simply seeing it as "just a job" or "work"—two other concepts that have, unfortunately, fallen on hard times within Christianity. If more talented Christians would make it their God-honoring ambition to make a difference in culture rather than merely criticizing it or retreating from it, then perhaps many fields that are now dominated by non-

Christian worldviews would begin to shift toward God rather than away from him.

Baptized Ambitions

We should seek to cultivate our God-given ambition for excellence. Diminishing the role of the arts is not the solution but part of the problem. Unfortunately, some Christians tend to view the arts as superfluous—unnecessary diversions that won't help anyone "make it," vocationally speaking, in this world. This needs to stop. God values artistic beauty and, with it, ambition that is properly focused in relation to it. What can we give to this world that is excellent and praiseworthy? We need to baptize our ambitions, converting them to Christ-driven desires that manifest themselves in wonderfully creative ways. As such, holiness and virtue must also play a part in relation to our ambitions.

Consider a world without ambition. What do you envision? Since ambition drives progress, a world without ambition would stagnate. What about a world without Christian ambition? Such a world would not only stagnate but also quite literally result in a dark age, deprived of both the love and the light of God. Yes, we must avoid the negative expressions of ambition driven by self-centeredness, but we also must redeem ambition, reclaiming it within a Christian understanding. In relation to culture, we were made to *make*, not just to *take*.

Properly applying ambition requires properly understanding our underlying motives. If we honestly ask ourselves what our motivation is in relation to our ambitions, what is the answer? If our immediate answer points back to ourselves, we need to give the matter some more thought. In addition, there is the danger of comparing ourselves to others. As Os Guinness has said, what matters is that we keep in mind "the audience of one"—that is, God.[2] What would God have us do to add something positive to culture?

Even if we are not artistically inclined, our ambitions in everyday life should reflect the character—indeed the virtues—of God. We need to see *all* of life as God-honoring, thereby avoiding the mistake of a dichotomy between the sacred and the secular. Ambition guided by love and by a pursuit of God's glory is the ideal. In relation to virtue, our moral lives should be about maturing our character, not achieving any particular material success.

Our ambitions may not be easy to achieve. In fact, they probably won't be. Assuming that something worth achieving should be easy is a misconception; in reality, it usually is difficult. Moral reformers— people who have made a real difference in culture and society— have not had it easy. Historically, these sorts of individuals are usually persecuted long before their actions make a difference.

Yes, Remy is just a computer-animated rat, but he can serve as an example of the difference we can make if we take the time to properly direct and pursue our ambitions.

Discussion Questions

1. What comes to mind when you think about the word *ambition*? What has shaped your perception of ambition?

2. List two or three examples of negative expressions of ambition. Why are these negative examples? Do the same for positive examples of ambition.

3. The Bible desires that we cultivate God-centered ambition rather than self-centered ambition. What are some dangers of self-centered ambition?

4. Think of an aspect of culture that you admire because of its excellence and creative contributions. What would that field look like without ambition driving it?

5. How does Remy the rat exemplify positive ambition?

6. What is your view of the relationship between Christianity and culture?

TECHNOLOGY

WALL-E—
"Everything you need to be happy."

WALL-E is on a quest. He has fallen in love with another robot, EVE, but something has gone wrong with her. The little robot's misadventures lead him on a journey through the wonders of space, where a survey ship he is riding finally docks with an enormous cruise ship, the *Axiom*. Built by the once-globally dominating corporation Buy n Large (BnL), the *Axiom* is a luxury starship designed to cater to every need of the humans on board. WALL-E, on the other hand, is a simple garbage-compacting robot. To be precise, he's a Waste Allocation Load Lifter—Earth Class (WALL-E), left behind on Earth hundreds of years earlier as part of a fleet of robots whose job was to clean up the vastly polluted planet. The trouble is that WALL-E is the only active robot of his kind left. After hundreds of years on Earth, he has developed something of a quirky personality, collecting various objects he finds in trash piles, befriending an invincible cockroach and watching the 1969 musical *Hello, Dolly!* over and over again. When the sleek robot

EVE arrives in search of something important, WALL-E is immediately smitten. Hitching a ride on the survey ship in his pursuit of EVE, WALL-E becomes the proverbial fish out of water and a reluctant hero.

After docking with the enormous *Axiom*, WALL-E meets only automated machinery and other robots. No human is in sight, since nearly all the tasks aboard the *Axiom* are automated. The *Axiom*, moreover, is sparkling clean, while WALL-E is old and dirty, causing a little *Axiom* robot named M-O (Microbe Obliterator) to pursue a mission of his own—cleaning up the mess WALL-E leaves wherever he goes. WALL-E makes it out of the docking bay and finds a "highway" filled with fast-moving robots of all kinds, busily going about their tasks. There are

ACTION!

WALL-E

U.S. Release Date: June 27, 2008

WALL-E features scenes and music from the 1969 film *Hello, Dolly!* When asked why he included this material, director Andrew Stanton replied, "When I got to *Hello, Dolly!* and I played 'Put on Your Sunday Clothes,' and that first phrase 'Out there' came out, it just fit musically. . . . I finally realized, 'You know what, this song is about two guys that are just so naïve, they've never left a small town, and they just wanna go out in the big city for one night and kiss a girl. That's my main character.'"[1] Another song, "It Only Takes a Moment," provides the romantic connection needed between the main character, WALL-E, and the robot EVE. In addition, *Hello, Dolly!* serves to ground the futuristic film in a reality to which viewers can more easily relate.

still no humans in sight. WALL-E enters the fray, causing something of a robot pileup in the process, and continues his pursuit of EVE. Finally, WALL-E encounters his first human, a large man wearing red and sitting in what appears to be a moving recliner (BnL "all-access hover-chairs"). Projected a short distance from his face is a computer screen. Soon WALL-E encounters thousands of other overweight humans, all wearing red and riding on identical automated recliners and all staring at a computer screen.

Every chair is moving rapidly, and every human is staring at a screen. No one is interacting with one another face-to-face—it's all online via a virtual world. If someone is thirsty, they merely summon a robot, who obediently brings them what they want. WALL-E looks up at a large domed ceiling and sees a computerized "sun," with the Buy n Large logo in it as the time and temperature are digitally reported beneath the logo. A calming female voice announces, "Buy n Large—everything you need to be happy. Your day is very important to us." Having left behind a desolate and polluted world, WALL-E now finds himself on a spaceship populated by technologically overrun humans.

Many reviews of the film *WALL-E* concentrated on its emphasis on the supposed evils of consumerism and the dangers of unchecked pollution. Some suggested that *WALL-E* is merely a "message movie" in favor of environmentalism and human responsibility to care for the planet. Yet underlying *WALL-E* are important concepts related to technology. As such, the focus of this chapter is on technology and, in particular, its relationship to virtue.

Thinking About Technology

We live in a world of technology, dominated by electronic gadgetry that inundates us with information, sounds and images on a regular basis. What is now commonplace, however, is still relatively new, historically speaking. The World Wide Web, used daily by billions of individuals, has only been a viable reality since 1993, and commercial cell phones entered the world in 1983. Whether we are on a camping trip, in a restaurant, on a family vacation or in a pew at church, it's now possible to instantly connect. The Internet never closes, and neither does technology. Every second of every day, a world of technology is available to us. But do we ever stop to give it serious consideration? Developing robust theologies and philosophies of technology are important, though often neglected, pursuits. Too many of us simply go with the flow of technology without taking a step back to think about it biblically or in relation to virtue.

Technology is not the same as scientific knowledge. Rather, technology applies scientific knowledge, using it to develop what are, hopefully, useful and practical tools. The clock, for instance, is technology, but the knowledge required to make one is not. The application of technology is also something to consider. Taking the clock as an example again, we can note that it was invented not by corporations eager to track work hours and to make money, but by monks, eager to better schedule their devotional days in the worship of God. The way we use technology matters. The Internet can communicate the gospel of Christ, but can also display pornography.

Does this mean that all technology is neutral? Not necessarily. Some would argue that certain kinds of technology are inherently suited for certain purposes. For example, television serves better as an entertainment device than as a useful tool for presenting deep discussion and discourse. In other words, different technologies bring with them "baggage" that is particularly tailored for certain tasks.

Technological discernment is needed, lest we become absorbed by the technology that is developing around us simply because it is there. This, in brief, is what developing a philosophy of technology is all about. A theology of technology, furthermore, will seek to understand technology within a biblical framework, applying what we know about God and his desire for how we live our lives to technology. As human beings made in God's image, we also possess sensibilities that may be disrupted by certain forms and uses of technology. The pursuit of technologically driven entertainment in particular often serves to divert and distract rather than edify and equip.

Having technological discernment does not mean that we bury our heads in the sand, shunning all forms of technology. This approach would be to *entrench* ourselves in an isolated Christian subculture. Another option is to *embrace* technology wholeheart-edly, using every bit of it as best we can as part of the Christian life. A third option is to intelligently *engage* technology, doing our best to remain "wise as serpents and innocent as doves" (Matthew 10:16). But intelligently engaging technology requires a founda-tional understanding of the rudiments of theology—who God is, who Christ is, who we are, what our purpose is as a Christian, and what it means to be salt and light in the world. This foundation will equip us to engage any form of technology in the world intel-ligently rather than passively or, worse, unreflectively.

At this juncture, it's important to keep in mind a point we ex-plored in chapter one, namely, while humanity has progressed in relation to technology and overall inventiveness, and while we continue to progress in this regard, when it comes to moral prog-ress we are in much the same situation as every generation that preceded us. That is to say, our "progress" in relation to virtue oc-curs only on an individual level. We inherit technological ad-vances simply by being born into cultures that have such technol-ogy, but we do not inherit a refined virtuous character. Certainly God has infused each of us with a moral center, which passages like Romans 2:14-15 make clear. These verses speak of the moral law being written on our hearts. It is up to us, however, relying on God's guidance, to seek to mature in virtue individually. (We can, of course, make a difference to the world by living virtuously or setting examples as moral reformers do.)

These are challenging concepts to absorb and even more chal-lenging to implement, particularly if we haven't spent any signifi-cant time considering the nature of technology. Let's take a bit of a break, then, and turn to some examples of technology in Pixar's films to get a better idea of the issues at hand.

Pixar's Technology

WALL-E isn't the only Pixar film to touch on the topic of technology. In *A Bug's Life*, Flik the ant invents a device for picking grain that he hopes will grant more leisure time to his colony. "Flik, we don't have time for this," explains a frustrated Princess Atta. "Exactly!" Flik replies. "We never have time to collect food for ourselves because we spend all summer harvesting for the [grasshopper] offering. But my invention will speed up production!" A scene in *Toy Story 2* demonstrates channel-surfing, as Hamm the piggy bank rapidly changes channels in order to find a commercial for Al's Toy Barn.

Monsters, Inc. offers more examples of technology as well as its impact on sensibilities. During a commercial for Monsters, Incorporated, the screen shows a human child sitting mesmerized before a television screen, while a monster narrator laments, "We know the challenge. The window of innocence is shrinking. Human kids are harder to scare." The implication is that children surrounded by the influence of multimedia technology have become desensitized. Randall, the villain in *Monsters, Inc.*, believes that technology will save Monsters, Incorporated, demonstrating a common misperception that the world will find its salvation in science and technology.

WALL-E World

WALL-E, however, remains Pixar's most overt look at technology and its potential impact on humanity. Futuristic films generally represent a utopian world or a dystopian one. In a utopian world, the future is completely bright and positive, while in a dystopian world, the future is dark and gritty. *WALL-E* presents a dystopian view, in that Earth is a desolate, trashed wasteland abandoned by humans. The film might *appear* to display a mixture of the utopian and dystopian, in that life aboard the *Axiom* is presented as a place where human beings live in leisure and have all their needs met by machines. There is no war or strife with other nations, and everything is hygienic and cared for.

But something's not quite right. While things look positive on the surface, lurking beneath the "utopia" of the *Axiom* is a dystopia where humans have failed in their stewardship of earth, have become lethargic and unproductive in relation to their God-given creativity, have diminished the value of family and personal relationships and have retreated into a technologically induced stupor. In this dystopia they are mindlessly living but not thriving spiritually, intellectually or creatively.

In relation to virtue, the world depicted in *WALL-E* is one in which there is little to no room for virtue. Identity is confused, since humans do nothing and see no real purpose to their lives other than hedonistic leisure. There is no real room for justice, because nothing ever goes wrong that can't be made right by machinery. Lasting and meaningful friendships suffer because all interactions take place in a virtual world rather than face-to-face and in person. Family ties are also severed, as the education of children is turned over to Buy n Large computers rather than to individuals, much less to parents. Moreover, where are the opportunities for courage, adventure and ambition? Such things are unheard of aboard the *Axiom*, since everything runs so smoothly via advanced technology. The apparent utopia is in reality a dystopia, resulting in humans who have become less than human.

Is WALL-E's world really all that bad? Some would disagree. What's wrong with relying on technology to provide us with more free time? Are virtual relationships any less satisfying than those we form in person? Seeking to "save time" via technological progress is not wrong per se. Two relevant questions include "How is technology saving us time?" and "What are we doing with the time we have gained?" Marshall McLuhan pointed out in the 1960s that every form of technology has what he terms *extensions* and *amputations*. We might look at these terms as gains and losses. The telephone, for instance, extends my voice so that I can speak to someone who may be thousands of miles away. But while the voice is extended and the ability to speak to people far away is gained, something is also lost. In the case of the telephone, we lose the unique dynamic of interaction that takes place in person. In *WALL-E*, human interaction occurs almost exclusively through computer screens, thus diminishing the sort of fellowship that can only come about via face-to-face interactions.

Consider, too, what we are doing with the supposed "free time" granted to us by technology. In the contemporary world, our free time is more often than not spent pursuing forms of entertainment, immersing ourselves in technological oblivion. How many of us grasp the free time we have to ponder the great philosophical questions of history, to expand our knowledge of God, to study classic literature or to interact on meaningful levels with other human beings in order to solve problems and make a real difference in the world?

Certainly some of us do. No one wants to point a finger at themselves, though we are too often quick to point a finger at others. My intent here is not to condemn free time granted to us by technology, nor to condemn anyone for not taking full advantage of the time given; rather, it is to consider what it is that we value and pursue with our time. Christians in particular should seek to make "the best use of the time" that we have (Ephesians 5:16), rather than frittering it away on pointless diversions. Rest and leisure have a place in the Christian life, but what kind of rest and leisure are we pursuing, and is it worthwhile?

More Information, Less Meaning

Of course, *WALL-E* is just a movie, right? In fact, it is a movie produced by technology and distributed (somewhat ironically, given the jabs at Buy n Large) by a megacorporation: Disney. The dystopian future of lethargic, overweight human beings with nothing better to do than sit in automated recliners watching computer screens is far-fetched, isn't it?

Indeed, that may be the underlying point of *WALL-E*. By exaggerating the possibilities of humanity dominated by technology, *WALL-E* may, in fact, be making a loose reductio ad absurdum argument. In logic, a reductio ad absurdum argument makes its point by showing how absurd and, in fact, ridiculous something is. In Latin, reductio ad absurdum literally means "to reduce something to an absurdity." What *WALL-E* demonstrates in this regard is the absurdity of living completely unproductive and meaningless lives supported by technological domination and saturation. And yet, how far off is the fictional world of *WALL-E* when compared to our own technologically saturated culture?

WALL-E also presents us with a world where there is no ambition. No one thinks meaningful thoughts, no one creates works of art, and no one contributes beauty or intellectual betterment. In short, a world dominated by technology is a world of human stagnation. It is not an Orwellian world, where some external oppressor forces an unhappy life on the people, as in *1984*. Rather, it is a Huxleyan world, as in *Brave New World*, in which human beings do not need an outside oppressor because they willingly drown themselves in technologically induced pleasures that stifle humanity.

What of relationships in a world saturated by technology? With the advent of the online world, social networking, mobile phones and other technologies, we have, more than ever before, the ability to stay connected and in touch with others. But what are we saying? Not much that is meaningful. As one thinker has said, "We live in a world where there is more and more information and less and less meaning."[2] Are we losing touch with what it means to be truly human, relationally, as God intended?

In *WALL-E*, technology has given humanity a means to escape responsibility. They have trashed the Earth and instead of facing up to their actions, they escape into space aboard a cruise ship. Has humanity done the same in the real world? Kicked out of the garden, we wander the planet in search of meaning, but rarely looking for it in the right place. Fortunately, the dystopian world of *WALL-E* is one where hope is regained and redemption is possible. The humans realize their mistakes and return to a battered Earth, ready to right what is wrong.

We need to take the time to think about technology in our lives, how we use it, its benefits and detriments, and how we might better integrate our views and uses of technology with sound theology. Consider the hyperlink mentality. Being able to read a document with links in it to other "pages" certainly has advantages, but also disadvantages. (Recall McLuhan's "extensions" and "amputations.") Can we still follow linear thought or read a book or follow a complex idea that relies on understanding important concepts along the way? Is our attention only caught by the sound bite rather than the sound idea? I don't pretend to have complete and definitive answers to these and related questions. But they are questions worth considering and questions that can help us grow in virtue in relation to how we use technology in our daily lives.

Cars features an amusing scene in which two lost tourists try to find their way through the sleepy town of Radiator Springs. Mini and Van are just passing through. When they are offered a map, Van replies, "We don't need anything, thank you very much. There's no need to ask for directions. . . . I know exactly where we're going. . . . I don't need a map, I have the GPS. Never need a map again. Thank you!" By the end of the film, however, after the credits have rolled, Mini and Van are lost in the desert. "Can we please ask someone for directions?" asks Mini. Their technology has failed them. How much do we rely on technology at the expense of common sense? How often do we think technology will "save" us, only to find that it leads us farther into the desert?

Discussion Questions

1. Buy n Large is depicted negatively as a global corporation obsessed with cultivating consumerism. How does technology

facilitate consumerism today? Can you provide some examples of consumerism made possible by contemporary technology? What's good about consumerism? What's bad?

2. *WALL-E* includes themes relevant to the stewardship of the Earth. How do ecological concerns fit into a Christian view of the world?

3. Most of us have had interactions with others via email and probably other forms of electronic communications such as text messaging, chats, Twitter, Facebook or MySpace. What about these forms of communication is the same as communicating in person? What about them is different?

4. How might you go about developing a philosophy of technology? What kinds of questions would you ask about the technologies you use regularly?

5. Think about a world without the Internet or telephones (landlines and cell phones) or, in fact, any kind of electronic technology whatsoever. How would you communicate with others? What benefits are there to the alternative forms of communications you would use? What detriments do they have?

6. Three approaches to technology were briefly outlined: to entrench ourselves, to embrace technology uncritically or to engage technology intelligently. Where do you see yourself falling within the spectrum of those three options?

LOVE

Up—
"I have just met you, and I love you!"

Carl and Russell are an unlikely duo on an adventure in South America, journeying to Paradise Falls. Carl is a grumpy old man on a quest to fulfill a dream his late wife had, while Russell is a young Asian American boy eager to earn a merit badge for assisting the elderly. Dug, on the other hand, is loyal, kind and eager to please. He's also a dog. While on their journey, Carl and Russell see from a distance the shape of what they believe to be a man. As they approach, it's apparent that what they've been looking at is actually a rock formation. Still, they are puzzled by the voice they have heard. A joyful dog bounds into the scene and, much to the surprise of Carl and Russell, begins not to bark but to speak! Some of Dug's first words to the strangers are, "I have just met you, and I love you!" Man's best friend has lived up to his reputation.

Pixar's tenth feature film, *Up,* is filled with deep themes, not the least of which is love. The main character, Carl Fredricksen, is motivated by love and responds by doing whatever it takes to

ACTION!

Up

U.S. Release Date: May 29, 2009

Diagnosed with vascular cancer, ten-year-old Colby Curtin desperately wanted to see one more Pixar film before she died. Too ill to go to the theater, a family member contacted Disney and Pixar to explain Colby's situation. The next day a Pixar employee arrived at Colby's home with a DVD copy of *Up*, which was still playing in theaters at the time, along with some other Pixar goodies such as stuffed animals and an adventure book similar to the one featured in *Up*. Colby got to see and enjoy the movie, but died later that night. "I'll have to fill those adventures in for her," said Colby's mother, Lisa.[1] If the power of story captivates us, as it did Colby, stories about love captivate us even more.

honor the memory of his wife, Ellie. In flipping through Ellie's adventure book (a scrapbook), Carl comes across a childhood drawing that Ellie made that depicts a house right on the edge of Paradise Falls. So that is what Carl decides to do: take their home to South America. And what better way to do so than by inflating thousands of balloons and taking off? Where does Carl go? Up, of course. It's only later that Carl flips through the rest of the scrapbook and finds a celebration of the life and love he shared with Ellie for so many years. He sees pictures of their joyous wedding celebration and other happy scenes from their life. "Thanks for the adventure," Ellie has written at the end. "Now go have a new one! Love, Ellie."

Having met her when they were children, Carl loved Ellie most of his life. Now that she is gone, he has become disgruntled and cantankerous. Will Carl's life ever matter again? What can he do to honor the love of his life? How does one go on following the death of a beloved spouse? While ostensibly a family film geared to children, *Up* grapples with many of these issues, but does so in a way that audiences have come to expect from Pixar. The film is not a stern lecture, and neither is it preachy. Instead, it does what Pixar often does best: it shows. Like *WALL-E*, the Pixar film that preceded it, *Up* excels in showing us scenes that move us deeply. We see the young and shy Carl, excited about adventure, as he meets the effervescent and fearless Ellie in her clubhouse (a broken-down house that eventually becomes the home of Carl and Ellie after their marriage).

In a montage that lasts just a few minutes, we see Carl and Ellie enjoying each other, going to work, trying to save money for their adventurous trip to South America and dealing with the challenges of everyday life. Carl is kind and, while still quiet, joyful. Love has given him the strength to face each day of his life, no matter how arduous. But now Ellie is gone and Carl is alone. Fortunately, love will once again motivate Carl. And so he goes up, accompanied unexpectedly by young Russell, and later joined by Dug, the lovable dog, as well as Kevin, a colorful and elusive bird.

The Virtue of Love

The word *love* is used in many different ways. We may love a certain flavor of ice cream, but we also love our spouse, our child and our good friend. We may place love in the category of emotion alone, separating it entirely from anything remotely having to do with the intellect. We may think we're in love, but in reality we're merely infatuated—a short-lived sort of passion. Misconceptions about love compound the challenge of defining it. If pop culture drives meaning, then love is in serious trouble; if it defines reality, then trouble becomes tragedy. More often than not, popular views of love lack both depth and truth.

Love is, in fact, a virtue. In Christian tradition and in biblical exposition, it is a key virtue: "So now faith, hope, and love abide, these three; but the greatest of these is love" (1 Corinthians 13:13). As such, love is foundational to Christian ethics. It is not an exaggeration to say that without love, Christianity collapses. Without God's love, Christianity cannot exist as it is intended. "God is love," read 1 John 4:8 and 16, meaning that God is not only loving, but that love is inherent in his very nature. If we are to grow in character and virtue, love is an essential part of the process. Just as godly ambition is not self-centered but God-centered and other-centered, so too is godly love. A foundational reason for Christianity's profound influence on history is that Christians are moved to action because of God's love. For Christians, love is much more than simply an abstract academic pursuit; it is living a virtuous life and demonstrating this by our actions.

Pixar's Love

When Pixar director Peter Docter had green, one-eyed monster Mike Wazowski plan a cozy dinner for two with his girlfriend Celia in *Monsters, Inc.*, he probably didn't anticipate anyone including the monstrous relationship as an example of romantic love. "Think romantical thoughts," says Mike as he leaves his love, Celia, who happens to be a snake-headed monster. In *The Incredibles*, former Supers Mr. Incredible and Elastigirl also express their love for one another: from playful banter while on "duty," to their wedding, to their life together fifteen years later, to their expressions of love for their children, it is clear that Bob and Helen are truly in love. Three Pixar films in particular, however, will serve as examples of love: *Finding Nemo*, *WALL-E* and *Up*.

Marlin and Nemo

Finding Nemo provides examples of family love, specifically love between a parent and child. Although Nemo's father, Marlin, is overprotective, he is driven not by a desire to control but by his love for Nemo. Marlin has undergone a traumatic event—the loss of his wife and his other children—and, as a result, is particularly careful with the life that has been entrusted to him via Nemo. Unknown to Marlin, on the first day of school Nemo's class is planning a field trip to the "drop off"—the very location where

Marlin lost his wife, Coral, and his other children. Marlin is understandably upset and follows Nemo to make sure he is safe, only to find his son experiencing some mild peer pressure to swim out to open water. Out of concern for Nemo, Marlin scolds him, only to have his son utter words that hurt every parent: "I hate you." When Nemo is captured by a diver, however, Marlin doesn't think twice about pursuing his son. Despite Marlin's fears of open water and anything even remotely dangerous, he overcomes his own limitations not for his sake but out of love for his son.

Fortunately, the time that Marlin and Nemo spend apart, which constitutes the bulk of the film, is not wasted. Both parent and child mature in their own ways during the ordeal of separation. Marlin learns that he can't control every aspect of Nemo's life, but instead has to learn to give his child room to enjoy life. Nemo, meanwhile, learns that even though he has a gimpy fin, he is still capable of accomplishing much. He also learns that his father truly loves him and will stop at nothing to rescue him.

While the director of *Finding Nemo*, Andrew Stanton, has said that the story is about faith overcoming fear, the film also offers an interesting parallel to God's love for us. After all, the Bible speaks of God as our Father, even providing stories about the love between a father and a son, such as the parable of the prodigal son. As 1 John 3:1 reads, "See what kind of love the Father has given to us, that we should be called children of God; and so we are." There's also the story of God the Father sending God the Son—Jesus Christ—to die for us, not for selfish reasons, but because "God so loved the world" (John 3:16).

WALL-E and EVE

WALL-E offers much to reflect on in relation to technology, consumerism and stewardship of the Earth, but it does so by telling us a love story. What's particularly interesting is that the love story is about two robots: WALL-E and EVE. Left on Earth for hundreds of years in order to fulfill his directive of compacting garbage, WALL-E has developed a quirky personality. He's naive, radiating a sort of childlike innocence. He learns about love by watching *Hello, Dolly!* Over and over again he plays a scene of a couple holding hands, and when he meets EVE, that's what he wants to do.

Two songs from *Hello, Dolly!* underscore the love theme of *WALL-E*. First is "Put on Your Sunday Clothes," which includes references to romantic love. The second is "It Only Takes a Moment." The song speaks of love as a solution to loneliness. A third song featured in *WALL-E*, "La Vie En Rose" ("Life Through Rose-Colored Glasses"), performed by Louis Armstrong, is also about romantic love and the enchantment it brings.

There is a certain longing to avoid being alone that is associated with romantic love. This is of interest in relation to the innate human desire for greater meaning and purpose. Christian thinkers such as Augustine, Blaise Pascal and C. S. Lewis have reasoned that this longing actually points to God and the reality of his existence. If all the human longings we are aware of do indeed have corresponding fulfillments based in reality, then by extension the human longing for meaning and purpose also has a source of fulfillment—God.

When WALL-E first sets eyes on EVE, he is not thinking about human longing or the existence of God as its fulfillment; that's not the goal of the film. Rather, *WALL-E* is a romantic love story along the lines of boy meets girl, girl is not interested in boy, but boy eventually wins over girl (in the case of *WALL-E*, it's robot boy meets robot girl). Nevertheless, the point is that *WALL-E* is essentially about love and the desire to pursue it. Challenges and setbacks are ultimately worth overcoming in order to find love.

Carl and Ellie

Up, as mentioned earlier, also features the theme of love. Unlike *Finding Nemo*, which emphasizes parental love, or *WALL-E*, which is about budding romantic love, *Up* touches on mature marital love. Carl, the main character, has spent most of his life with his wife, Ellie, but has lost her late in life. There are indeed differences between the love of a parent for a child, budding romantic love and the mature love between Carl and Ellie. We often focus so much on the feelings of love, which are indeed admirable and joyful, but fail to look at love in broader terms. In addition, contemporary pop culture's understanding of love is often shallow, failing to move beyond the feelings love stirs within us. Imitating our consumer-driven culture, we begin to treat relationships like we treat fads—they come and go, they interest us for a while then we move on to something else and dispose of them when they are no longer convenient. This approach, however, warps love, cheapening it rather than seeking to understand it on deeper levels.

Contrast this consumer-oriented, shallow approach to love with the joyous, mature love that can grow over the course of a lifetime, like that portrayed by Carl and Ellie in *Up*. Carl and Ellie have stuck with one another through the ups and downs of life: financial challenges, the inability to have children, and unfulfilled hopes and dreams. Through it all, they have one another. But something happens. Time catches up to all of us and in the case of Carl and Ellie, it catches her first. What is Carl to do without his beloved? He becomes bitter and lonely, and begins merely surviving rather than truly living. Finally, after a wild adventure, Carl realizes that all along Ellie considered their love the most wonderful adventure of all.

In an age of consumer-oriented relationships, the heartbreak of divorce and misperceptions about the meaning of love, *Up* is inspiring. Two people, Carl and Ellie, have joined together for a lifetime of love. They are wholeheartedly committed to one another, and the only thing that can separate them is death. As powerful as love is in a marriage relationship, it is merely a shadow of God's love for us. As Paul wrote, "Who shall separate us from the love of Christ? Shall tribulation, or distress, or persecution, or famine, or nakedness, or danger, or sword? . . . No, in all these things we are more than conquerors through him who loved us. For I am sure that neither death nor life, nor angels nor rulers, nor things present nor things to come, nor powers, nor height nor depth, nor anything else in all creation, will be able to separate us from the love of God in Christ Jesus our Lord" (Romans 8:35, 37-39).

The Greatest Commandment

When Jesus is asked, "Which is the great commandment in the Law?" he replies not by quoting one of the Ten Commandments but with two responses that both center on love: "You shall love the Lord your God with all your heart and with all your soul and with all your mind. This is the great and first commandment. And a second is like it: You shall love your neighbor as yourself. On these two commandments depend all the Law and the Prophets" (Matthew 22:36-40). The twofold reply emphasizes love of God as paramount, followed by love of others. Some commentators have noted that the first part of Christ's response summarizes the first part of the Ten Commandments, focusing on our relationship to God, while the second part of the response summarizes the second part of the commandments, focusing on our relationship to others.

How are we to love God? With our entire being. Love of God is not purely emotional, and neither is it purely intellectual. Instead, it encompasses our whole being. Too often we lack balance in this area. Some of us lean heavily in the direction of emotion, while others lean heavily on the intellect. But every aspect of our nature, made in God's image, is required if we are to truly love God as Christ intends. God made us to think and feel deeply, but thinking and feeling must move us to action. Living in a world of so many needs, we tend to focus only on ourselves and our own needs. Yet living virtuously is not about reaching a certain level of spiritual maturity and staying there. We must struggle, sometimes daily, to make the right choices.

In *Up*, Dug the dog loves everyone. He lacks the capacity to do much about it, however, other than slobbering on others, jumping on them or wagging his tail. Granted, he's a computer-animated dog, so he does possess some heroic traits that end up helping Carl and Russell; but Dug's range of virtue and love is limited by his nature. Human beings, on the other hand, are made in God's image. As such, we have extensive capacities for greatness, virtue and love—for making a positive difference in the world not for selfish reasons but for selfless ones. God's love should drive our every thought and action. We are fallen beings, so we usually fall short of this ideal; as Christians, however, we rely on God to see us through. We are not powerless to influence the world, but rather we are powerful when we rely on God's love.

Discussion Questions

1. How does the relationship between Carl and Ellie in *Up* represent mature love?

2. Think about the word *love* and how it is used in popular culture. What aspects of love does pop culture emphasize? Are the areas of emphasis different from biblical love? How so?

3. Love is a foundational Christian virtue. Why is this the case?

4. Can you relate to Marlin's love for Nemo? Can you relate to Nemo's love for Marlin? How is family love different from romantic love?

5. What do you think of using human longing and desire as a case

for the reality of God? What strengths and weaknesses does this approach have?

6. Jesus says to love God "with all your mind" (Matthew 22:37). How do you interpret the requirement to love God with your mind? How might that look?

CONCLUSION

The wisdom of Pixar is found in its virtues and expressed through story. Whether it is through toys who come alive, bugs who seek justice, cars that embark on unexpected adventures or futuristic robots that find love, Pixar films move and entertain us. Even though the movies are highly imaginative, deep down we can relate to the characters and their circumstances.

By watching Pixar films, we see stories vividly come to life. These stories are rooted in the human experience as well as in virtue. The very fabric of the moral universe contains an understanding of justice, courage, love and more, and, as a result, we resonate with these ideas. But where did this moral fabric come from, and who is the weaver? The Christian answer is found in God. As Creator and Designer, God is the foundation of moral truth, and the virtue of love is the cornerstone of Christian ethics. It is not surprising, then, that God, too, tells stories. We read in the pages of the Bible about justice, friendship, family, courage, adventure, love and other virtues. In the New Testament, we read intently as Jesus shares not formulas or complicated academic evaluations or presentations of ethics but stories that captivate us.

Our culture, too, is full of stories. As we "live and move and have our being" in God (Acts 17:28), so too we live, move and have our being in culture. Interaction with culture is unavoidable. Even if we try to escape it, culture has a way of finding us. But our purpose as Christians is not merely to take or consume culture; we must also seek to understand our culture and to participate in building it up in positive ways.

Our call is not to entrench ourselves, thus avoiding all aspects of culture, and neither is it to fully embrace and celebrate every aspect of culture without applying discernment. Instead, we are to engage culture intelligently. Moreover, in 2 Peter 1:5 we read, "make every effort to supplement your faith with virtue." We are to strive for moral excellence and to grow in spiritual maturity—not out of selfish ambition, but out of love for God that naturally flows into love for others.

"To infinity and beyond!" is Buzz Lightyear's clarion call to action. The call of the Christian is to love God and others. By doing so, we can make eternal differences in lives, to infinity and beyond.

APPENDIX A

Pixar's Plots

This appendix provides a brief summary of the ten Pixar films featured in this book. The summaries are not intended to replace in any way the actual experience of watching the films, but rather are intended to serve as a refresher for those who have seen the films. Readers who have not seen the films are encouraged to watch them; the summaries that follow contain spoilers.

Toy Story

The first entirely computer-generated feature film, *Toy Story* quickly won over audiences following its 1995 release. The plot centers on a group of toys belonging to a boy named Andy and his sister Molly. When humans are not around, the toys come to life. Andy's favorite toy is Woody, a cowboy doll. For his birthday, Andy is given a new toy—Buzz Lightyear. Unlike the other toys who know they are toys, Buzz believes he really is the Space Ranger that he is supposed to represent. Woody is displaced as Andy's favorite toy and becomes jealous. A series of mishaps results in

Woody and Buzz ending up in the hands of Sid, a boy who enjoys "torturing" toys. The two rival toys become friends, escape Sid and his vicious dog Scud, and return to their rightful roles as Andy's toys.

A Bug's Life

Released in 1998, *A Bug's Life* centers on the plight of a colony of ants oppressed by a gang of grasshoppers headed by Hopper. One ant, however, is determined to make a difference. Flik decides to leave the ant colony and look for help. He comes across a group of out-of-work circus bugs, mistakes them for warriors and returns with them to the colony. When the circus bugs realize the mistake they are eager to leave, but a series of events convinces them to stay with the colony. Princess Atta is suspicious of Flik but is swayed by a display of heroism on the part of the circus bugs and, later, a plan to construct a fake bird in order to scare the grasshoppers away. When the true identity of the circus bugs is revealed, the ants are shocked and terrified. The grasshoppers return, but Flik implements the original plan, launching the fake bird. Hopper is attacked by a real bird, and the grasshopper gang flees.

Toy Story 2

This 1999 sequel to *Toy Story* finds Woody stolen by toy collector Al, who intends to sell a toy collection featuring Woody to a museum in Japan. Woody discovers he was based on a famous television show, *Woody's Roundup*. New toys introduced include Stinky Pete ("The Prospector"), Jessie the yodeling cowgirl, and the horse Bullseye. Andy's toys, headed by Buzz Lightyear, seek to rescue Woody, but when they find him, Woody decides to stay and become part of the museum in Japan. Later, however, Woody has a change of heart and determines that the best place for him is where he can bring joy to Andy, regardless of how long the happiness will last. Trapped in a suitcase on an airport conveyor belt, Andy's toys once again seek to rescue Woody. Stinky Pete is defeated and Woody, Jessie and Bullseye return to Andy's house, along with the rest of the toys, from the rescue mission.

Monsters, Inc.

Monsters, Inc., released in 2001, is based on the premise that a world of monsters, whose job it is to scare children, really exists. The monsters are just doing their jobs, collecting energy from children's screams in order to power their world. Sulley is the top "scarer," aided by his one-eyed assistant Mike Wazowski. They view children as toxic. When one little girl, nicknamed Boo, enters the monster world, the Child Detection Agency begins an investigation of Monsters, Inc. It is discovered that a competing scarer, a lizard-like monster named Randall, is involved in a plot to kidnap children and forcibly extract screams from them. Henry J. Waternoose, a crab-like creature and head of the company, is also involved in the plot. When they discover the plot, Sulley and Mike are banished to the human world, but they return in order to rescue Boo and to reveal Waternoose's plans. Laughter, it is discovered, is much more powerful than screams. As a result, the "scare floor" becomes the "laugh floor," and monsters make children laugh in order to collect energy.

Finding Nemo

Pixar's underwater adventure *Finding Nemo* awed audiences in 2003 with its amazing visual effects and touching story. A clownfish named Marlin loses his wife and all but one of his children to a barracuda attack. Consequently, Marlin becomes an overprotective father, obsessed with keeping his son Nemo safe. On his first day of school, Nemo is captured by a diver, a dentist who adds Nemo to his office fish tank. Desperate to find Nemo, Marlin embarks on an adventure worthy of Odysseus; the clownfish and his new companion, a forgetful Dory, encounter sharks, jellyfish, sea turtles, a whale and more on their journey to find Nemo. Meanwhile, Nemo's fish tank companions, including a seasoned fish named Gill, plan their escape. Marlin and Nemo are ultimately reunited, with Marlin having learned to enjoy being a father without being overprotective.

The Incredibles

The ambitious 2004 film *The Incredibles* features Pixar's first cast of characters based entirely on human beings. The premise grants the reality of superheroes, but finds them living underground and anonymously, having been forced by the government to cease their often havoc-creating activities. The story centers on the Parr family. Bob is formerly Mr. Incredible, capable of superhuman strength, while his wife Helen used to be Elastigirl, capable of stretching her body great distances. Their three children include the shy teenager Violet, who is able to create force fields and turn invisible; Dash, who can run at great speeds; and baby Jack-Jack, who has yet to manifest any powers. Bob is unsatisfied with his boring insurance company job and longs for the glory days of being a superhero. His nemesis is Syndrome, a former fan of Mr. Incredible who is now systematically exterminating superheroes. When Mr. Incredible uncovers Syndrome's plans to attack a city with a powerful robot called an Omnidroid, he intervenes but is captured. Mr. Incredible's family arrives to rescue him and, together, they defeat the Omnidroid and Syndrome.

Cars

Although the 2006 film *Cars* received more negative reviews than any Pixar film to date, overall the movie was a box office success and the second-highest-grossing film of the year. The story centers around a cocky rookie race car named Lightning McQueen and his fixation on winning the Piston Cup. An unexpected detour finds Lightning under arrest in the largely forgotten town of Radiator Springs, off Route 66. At first Lightning is angry and frustrated and misses the fast-paced lifestyle he was used to, but in time he learns to enjoy the town and its quirky residents, such as the tow truck Mater, Doc Hudson, Sarge the Jeep and Fillmore the hippie. Lightning falls in love with Sally, a Porsche. Eventually Lightning emerges from seclusion to race in the Piston Cup, but he misses his friends. Doc Hudson and some of the other residents of Radiator Springs arrive to encourage and help Lightning win the race. In the end, Lightning loses the race because he stops to help another car that is having difficulty, but he wins friendship and gains a deeper understanding of what is important in life.

Ratatouille
Some critics and fans were wary of 2007's *Ratatouille*, featuring rats as main characters, but in the end the film won over both audiences. Remy is a rat who wants to be a chef. Linguini is an awkward young man working as a garbage boy in a famous Parisian restaurant, Gusteau's. The two are brought together, and Linguini soon discovers that Remy is an excellent chef. Hiding under Linguini's hat, Remy is able to control the human and thus realize his dream of being a chef. The head chef, Skinner, is suspicious and also jealous of Linguini's success, particularly after he discovers that Linguini is actually the son of deceased chef Gusteau. Linguini falls in love with Colette, another ambitious chef working at Gusteau's, and begins to take Remy for granted. Remy, resentful of this turn of events, returns to his rat colony and plans to raid Gusteau's food pantry. When the kitchen staff discover that Linguini has been relying on a rat to prepare the meals, they abandon him (except for Colette, who returns). The rats, directed by Remy, prepare ratatouille for the famous restaurant critic, Anton Ego, who is delighted. When Gusteau's is closed by health inspectors, Linguini, Remy and Colette open a new restaurant: Ratatouille.

WALL-E

Moving from rats to robots, Pixar released *WALL-E* in 2008. The main character is a garbage-compacting robot whose name is derived from the acronym Waste Allocation Load Lifter—Earth Class. Having spent hundreds of years working on cleaning up Earth, WALL-E has developed a quirky personality, collecting various objects of interest and watching the 1969 film *Hello, Dolly!* When the robot EVE arrives looking for plant life and encounters WALL-E, first she ignores him and later accepts him as her friendly companion. EVE finds a plant, and a spaceship arrives to take her back to the *Axiom*, a large cruise ship–like vessel that is home to all the descendants of humans who left Earth hundreds of years earlier. Someone steals the plant before it can be tested, so EVE and WALL-E begin looking for the plant. Believing that Earth would never again be habitable, the president of Buy n Large, a global consumer powerhouse, had instructed the *Axiom's* computers not to return to Earth; now that plant life has been found, however, the captain realizes that it's not only safe to return but that it is their duty as humans to do so. WALL-E finds the plant, but the robot is severely damaged. Returning to Earth on the *Axiom*, EVE finds spare parts for WALL-E and revives him. They hold hands, thus realizing WALL-E's dream of companionship and love from watching *Hello, Dolly!*

Up

The poignant 2009 film *Up* tells the tale of Carl Fredricksen, his fascination as a child with adventure hero Charles Muntz, Fredricksen's marriage to his childhood sweetheart Ellie, their life together, Ellie's eventual death and Carl's quest to travel to South America in order to honor Ellie's desire to visit the mythic Paradise Falls. Now an elderly man, Carl has become grumpy and cantankerous. He is befriended by Russell, a young boy and Wilderness Explorer seeking to earn a merit badge. Carl inflates thousands of balloons that lift his home into the air. Unbeknown to Carl, Russell is on the porch and, consequently, comes along for the fantastic voyage. They arrive in South America but must journey even farther to reach Paradise Falls. Meanwhile, adventurer Charles Muntz has spent years of his life in the South American jungle, supposedly missing but in reality seeking to capture a rare bird. Muntz is waited on by his trained dogs, which are capable of speaking via special collars. Befriended by the friendly dog Dug, Carl and Russell travel through the jungle and encounter various obstacles—including Muntz, who believes they are really interested in capturing the elusive bird. Carl and Muntz battle aboard the airship *Spirit of Adventure*, with Muntz ultimately falling to his doom. Carl and Russell return home safely, with Carl transformed for the better as a result of the adventure.

APPENDIX B

Pixar's Short Films

Full-length Pixar movies are usually prefaced by short Pixar films. What follows are summaries of the ten short films that either accompanied the theatrical release of a Pixar feature film or were included as bonuses or special features on retail versions of the feature films. Additional Pixar short films are available on DVD and Blu-Ray as *Pixar Short Films Collection, Volume 1*, and on iTunes.

Tin Toy
Bundled as a bonus feature with the *Toy Story* VHS and DVD releases in 2000, *Tin Toy* is a 1988 Pixar short film that won an Academy Award in the category of Animated Short Film. It tells the story of a one-man band tin toy named Tinny. The toy is eager to be played with by a baby until he sees how the slobbering child behaves (sucking on toys, shaking them, breaking them, dropping them, etc.). Tinny wants to get away from the baby, but every time the tin toy moves, the musical instruments attached to him make

sounds. The baby pursues Tinny, who escapes under a couch where he finds many other cowering toys. When the baby falls and begins to cry, Tinny feels sorry for him and emerges, successfully cheering up the baby, who eventually decides to play with Tinny's box and a paper bag instead. The roles are now reversed, with Tinny following the baby and wanting to be played with, while the baby wanders off with the large paper bag on his head.

The film is remarkable not only for its advanced use of the technology of the day but also for once again demonstrating Pixar's ability to bring inanimate objects to life so convincingly. In addition, although *Tin Toy* is only a few minutes long, it encapsulates the core story idea for *Toy Story*—toys that are alive and that wish for nothing more than to be played with and to bring joy to their owners.

Geri's Game

This 1997 short film accompanied the theatrical release of *A Bug's Life*. It tells the story of an eccentric elderly man named Geri, who plays a spirited game of chess against himself in a park. Each player, played by Geri, has distinctive features and mannerisms. One is confident, aggressive, boastful and secure in his belief that he will win the chess game, while the other is reserved, overly cautious, sheepish and fearful of losing. During the course of the game, the "camera" moves from one of Geri's personalities to the other, creating a realistic-looking competition among them. In the end, the sheepish Geri, when he is about to lose, feigns a weak heart and dramatically collapses beneath the table. The confident Geri is confused. Sheepish Geri emerges and quickly spins the chessboard around to his advantage. As a result, sheepish Geri wins the game and demands the victory prize: his false teeth.

The character of Geri appears briefly in *Toy Story 2* as the toy cleaner who spruces up Woody. Story-wise, *Geri's Game* is endearing in its presentation of an elderly man who is aware that he is only playing against himself but who has not lost his childlike wonder or enjoyment of life.

Luxo Jr.

Although it is not Pixar's first short film, it is most recognizable because one of the characters in it is the lamp in the studio's logo, which bounces on the "i" in Pixar and replaces the letter. Made in 1986, Luxo Jr. later played in 1999 with Toy Story 2. The story is simple but captivating. It features two Luxo-style lamps, one intended to depict a parent, and the other smaller lamp a child. The film has no dialogue, only an upbeat jazzy soundtrack and sound effects. What is remarkable is the animation that makes inanimate objects into believable characters with distinct personalities. Luxo Jr. plays with a ball, but soon it deflates, leaving him dejected. He returns with a larger ball, just as eager to play as before, while the adult lamp shakes its head.

For the Birds

The 2000 short film For the Birds accompanied the theatrical release of Monsters, Inc. It tells the story of a flock of small, cliquish birds relaxing on a power line. A larger bird of another species appears and is mocked by the flock. The larger bird ignores the mocking and flies over to the flock, landing on the power line in the middle of them. The power line dips due to the weight of the large bird. The smaller birds peck the larger one's feet until he is hanging precariously upside down, although he remains unaware of the harm the smaller birds are trying to do to him. The shot widens, and we that see the larger bird's head is almost touching the ground. The smaller birds realize their mistake too late and are sprung into the air, losing their feathers in the process. The larger bird is now sitting on the ground as the smaller birds land, featherless, around him. The larger bird laughs while the smaller birds hide behind him.

The lesson is quite simple: don't make fun of those who are different from you.

Knick Knack

Featured with *Finding Nemo*, the 1989 short film *Knick Knack* is about a snowman trapped in a snow globe who wants to escape. The star of the film tries again and again to break out of his snow-globe prison using various methods, including explosives. The catchy soundtrack was provided free of charge by Bobby McFerrin. Eventually as a result of the snowman using explosives to break out, the snow globe falls off a shelf, and the snowman notices an emergency exit. He exits the globe but realizes he has landed in a fishbowl and sees a mermaid nearby. As he prepares to walk toward her, the snow globe floats over the snowman and he is once again trapped.

Boundin'

Featuring narration by Pixar employee Bud Luckey, who directed the film, the 2003 short *Boundin'* was featured with *The Incredibles*. The film features a joyful dancing lamb who, after being sheared, is dejected. A mythical jackelope (a rabbit with the horns of a deer) appears and cheers him up. The lamb learns to live with his regular shearing and remain joyful in his bounding. Told as a sort of ballad, there is more dialogue in this short Pixar film than in most. The underlying message may be interpreted as persevering despite the setbacks and challenges of life, as well as communicating a general enthusiasm for life. The lamb literally and figuratively weathers the storms of life. There is also a suggestion of accepting one's identity. A theme-park atmosphere permeates the film, as prairie dogs, fish and an owl bounce about the scenery.

One Man Band

Pixar's 2005 short film *One Man Band* was shown along with *Cars*.

The story features only three characters: a plucky peasant girl, a one-man band featuring primarily percussion and a horn section, and a one-man band featuring primarily strings. The little girl approaches a fountain, planning to toss a coin in it, but is swayed by the brass musician to give him the coin. As she prepares to do so, she hears the string player and wanders over to his side. The two musicians then begin an increasingly fevered musical battle to win the heart and coin of the little girl. A variety of musical styles are represented, including classical, jazz and more (the score was composed by Michael Giacchino, who also composed the inspiring film scores for *The Incredibles, Ratatouille* and *Up*). The musical frenzy that ensues causes the little girl to lose her coin down a drain. After obtaining a violin, the girl plays like a virtuoso and after only a few seconds, a passerby drops a large bag of coins in front of her. The musicians are stunned. The little girl teases them with two coins, then throws them into the air; they land in the top level of the fountain. The clever film closes with both musicians working together in an attempt to reach the two coins.

Lifted

The 2006 film *Lifted* was shown in conjunction with *Ratatouille*. It features two aliens in a spaceship: Mr. B, seasoned at the abduction of human beings, and an inexperienced student named Stu. The small, inexperienced alien continuously fumbles the abduction of the human, Ernie, by pressing the wrong switches that control the beam of light that is drawing the sleeping human to them. The film contains no dialogue; consequently, the entire story is driven by visuals, sounds and character expressions. Eventually the experienced alien has to take over in order to avoid catastrophe. The small alien is dejected, so the larger alien makes it up to him by allowing him to fly the ship. Stu crashes the ship directly over the human house. Fortunately the human survives and the ship flies off. If viewers look closely under the human's bed, they'll see that hidden in the shadows is Tinny, from the short film *Tin Toy*.

Presto

Shown with *WALL-E*, the 2008 short film *Presto* is about a magician, Presto DiGiotagione, and his hungry rabbit, Alec Azam. *Presto DiGiotagione* is apparently a play on the word *prestidigitation*, meaning "quick fingers" or "sleight of hand," while the rabbit's name is reminiscent of the magic word *alakazam*. Presto forgets to feed Alec a carrot before a performance, thus placing the rabbit in an uncooperative mood. Two magic hats are the center of Presto's act, with one hat acting as a portal to the other hat, resulting in many clever exploits of this unique and magical feature. Alec repeatedly fails to cooperate with Presto's act, causing him frustration and much pain; Presto ends up being injured by a mousetrap, a ladder, the shock of an electric current and more. As Presto is plummeting to his death, Alec has a change of heart and, using the magical hats, rescues the magician. In the process, Presto has performed an amazing feat and is applauded. The film ends with Alec finally getting his carrot.

Partly Cloudy

Appropriately shown before *Up*, the 2009 film *Partly Cloudy* is not so much about storks delivering babies as it is about the clouds that make the babies. Happy clouds create cuddly babies of all kinds, including puppies and kittens. The cloud Gus, however, is "partly cloudy," and the babies he makes are all dangerous creatures such as crocodiles and sharks. The stork assigned to Gus, named Peck, is constantly being injured by the babies that Gus makes. At one point, Peck flies away from Gus, apparently too terrified to continue delivering such dangerous babies. Gus cries, causing a thunderstorm. Peck returns, having asked another cloud to craft for him a football helmet and shoulder pads. Gus cheers up and immediately provides Peck with an electric eel to deliver. The story may not contain as much depth as some Pixar films, but it's not too much of a stretch to say that the underlying message is that true friendship perseveres despite challenges.

APPENDIX C

Movie Discussion Guide

This movie discussion guide covers all ten movies addressed in *The Wisdom of Pixar*. The guide may be used in small groups, youth groups, family settings, etc. Prior to delving into the discussion questions, watch the movie or read a summary of it (see appendix A).

Toy Story

1. Buzz seemed fairly happy thinking he was a real Space Ranger. Would he have been better off not knowing the truth about his identity as a toy? Why? Why not?

2. *Toy Story* features a lot of classic toys such as Mr. Potato Head, Battleship, a fire engine, Lincoln Logs, toy soldiers, Barrel of Monkeys, Tinkertoys, an Etch a Sketch and more. Did you ever play with any of these toys in your childhood? Which one did you like the best? Why? Compared to modern electronic toys, how well do the classic toys hold up in terms of their creativity and entertainment value?

3. Woody is jealous of Buzz because Andy is giving more attention to his new space toy than to Woody. The Bible refers to God as "a jealous God" (see, for example, Exodus 20:5; 34:14; Deuteronomy 4:24; 5:9; 6:15; Joshua 24:19). What do you think that means? If you're not sure, first spend some time reading the passages referenced and then discuss it some more.

4. Woody and Buzz start off as rivals but end up as friends. What brings them together? What keeps them together? Think of some good friends you have right now. How did you meet? Why do you remain friends?

5. Changing deeply held beliefs or worldviews (the way people look at and interpret the world) can take a lot of time. Buzz initially thinks that he is a real Space Ranger, but when confronted with clear evidence to the contrary in the form of the Buzz Lightyear television commercial, he is still not immediately convinced. Think about a worldview like atheism, which denies the existence of God. What kind of evidence would it take to convince an atheist that God exists? Would this likely be a quick process of change or a slow one? Why?

A Bug's Life

1. Some people don't like creepy crawly bugs at all. How did Pixar make the friendly bugs in A Bug's Life appealing? What did the filmmakers do to the mean bugs like the grasshoppers to make them less appealing? Do your answers reference appearance, behavior or other traits? Why is that?

2. Princess Atta is learning to become the new ant queen, while Flik is a simple worker ant trying to make a difference. Heimlich the caterpillar can't wait to transform into a butterfly, while Slim is bothered by always being cast as a stick, sword or other stick-like object. Tuck and Roll, the pill bugs, seem rather

oblivious to what is going on around them, presumably because they don't speak English but also because they have mischievous personalities. Of the characters listed or others in the movie, which one do you most identify with? Which one do you least identify with? Why?

3. The circus bugs are entertainers and, as such, enjoy making others happy. In our world, entertainment is big business. From television to motion pictures to music artists and video games, entertainment is all around us. Who are some entertainers you appreciate? Why?

4. The grasshoppers are bullies, living off the fear they create in others. The ants, inspired by Flik, eventually rebel. At what point is it right to rebel? Acts 5:29 reads, "We must obey God rather than any men." Read the passage in context and discuss what the phrase means. In what contexts should Christians obey God rather than human authorities?

5. Justice is a key theme in *A Bug's Life*. The ants are wrongfully oppressed by the grasshoppers. Name some injustices you are aware of in the world today. If you can't think of any, consider recent or recurring items in the news. What is the standard for determining what is just and what is unjust, what is fair and what is unfair? What can you do to actively make a difference in relation to something you find unjust?

Toy Story 2

1. So far Pixar has released three *Toy Story* feature films. Which one is your favorite? Why do you like it better than the others? If Pixar ever decides to make a *Toy Story 4*, what would you like to see in it?

2. What did you think of the bloopers at the end of *Toy Story 2*?

What about them did you find amusing?

3. Randy Newman's song, "You've Got a Friend in Me," is important in *Toy Story* and *Toy Story 2*. What is it about friendship that draws our interest? Think of someone you've been friends with longer than anyone else. How has your friendship grown over the years? Do you still think you will be friends many years from now?

4. There are at least three main villains in *Toy Story 2*: Al of Al's Toy Barn, "Stinky" Pete and Emperor Zurg. What characteristics make for a convincing villain? Even good characters sometimes do things that are not good. Is human nature basically good, basically bad or a mixture of both? Explain your answer.

5. *Toy Story 2* says a lot about friendship. Woody's friends are willing to place themselves in danger to help him, for instance. What traits do you value most in a friend? What traits do you value least?

Monsters, Inc.

1. *Monsters, Inc.* is about two everyday workers who also happen to be monsters. They live in the big city of Monstropolis and wear "odorant" instead of deodorant. Even though it's their job to scare kids, in reality it's the monsters who are afraid of children. What about this scenario makes for an interesting movie? How does looking at things or ideas from different or even opposing perspectives help us?

2. Mike and Sulley are two very different kinds of monsters, not only in appearance but in personality. How would you describe the personality of Mike, the one-eyed monster? How would you describe Sulley's personality? Are you more like Mike or Sulley?

3. Initially, Mike and Sulley are afraid of Boo because they are concerned she will contaminate them with her "toxic" presence. After all, Mike and Sulley have grown up being taught that the human world is toxic to the monster world. It takes time for them to realize that Boo is nothing like what they were taught about humans. What does this example say about prejudice? How are prejudices formed, and what can we do to overcome them?

4. Mr. Waternoose, the CEO of Monsters, Incorporated, initially comes across as a caring executive who wants the best for his company and for the city of Monstropolis. Later it is revealed that he's in league with Randall in using the "scream extractor" to increase power gained from scaring children. Do the ends ever justify the means? In other words, are there ever cases where doing wrong can turn out right?

5. At one point in the movie, Mike, Sulley and Boo have to travel to a number of closet doors in order to escape Randall. They visit all sorts of places including Japan, an island paradise and more. If you could step through a portal and find yourself in a different part of the world, where would you want to go? Why?

6. The movie concludes with a new Monsters, Incorporated, founded not on the motto "We scare because we care," but on the fact that laughter is supposedly ten times more powerful than fear. "Laughter is the best medicine" is a common saying. What is it about humor that human beings find interesting and enjoyable? What kinds of things make you smile or laugh?

Finding Nemo

1. If you are a parent, is your parenting style more like Marlin the clownfish or Crush the sea turtle? Marlin starts out being very overprotective of Nemo, while Crush is quite relaxed. If you're

not a parent, do you see your own parents as more like Marlin or Crush? If you become a parent at some point, would you want to be more like Marlin or Crush? How might their different parenting styles blend into something that's better than each style on its own?

2. The three sharks—Bruce, Anchor and Chum—are desperately trying to change from being meat-eaters to vegetarians. Despite their efforts, Bruce smells blood and once again becomes a fierce flesh-eating shark—at least until he recovers. Why is it difficult to change habits? In Romans, the apostle Paul writes about his inner struggle between what he would like to do and what he sometimes does even though he doesn't want to (see Romans 7:7-25). How can Christians overcome such inner struggles?

3. Mr. Ray is an energetic teacher, passionate about knowledge and teaching and genuinely interested in helping kids learn about the world around them. Consider a favorite teacher you have had. What made that teacher special? What traits did that teacher have that you would like to build up in yourself?

4. Family is important in *Finding Nemo*. Marlin truly loves Nemo and wants the best for him; he is willing to risk his life to be reunited with his son. But that doesn't mean that Marlin and Nemo always get along. How can family challenges help us to become better people?

5. Dory is a carefree fish, eager to try new things, while Marlin is just the opposite—full of worry and preferring to keep to what is safe and familiar. Are you more like Dory or Marlin? How much risk should we be willing to take in order to have fun?

The Incredibles

1. The Supers in *The Incredibles* have all sorts of powers: super

strength (Mr. Incredible), the ability to stretch great distances (Elastigirl), the ability to run fast (Dash), the capacity to create force fields and become invisible (Violet), and the power to freeze moisture in the air (Frozone). If you were a superhero, what sorts of powers would you like to have? Feel free to think beyond the powers in *The Incredibles*. Why would you want those powers? What would you do with them?

2. Is it Mr. Incredible's fault that Buddy (aka Syndrome) turned out the way he did? How might Mr. Incredible have better handled the situation with his admiring fan Buddy? Words are powerful. Read James 3:1-12. To what does James compare the tongue? What can you do to be more careful about what you say?

3. The Supers in *The Incredibles* are courageous. They don't stop to go over all the little ethical details of their behavior; instead, like Frozone when he sees the Omnidroid, they just react. What can you do in your life to help build up the virtue of courage?

4. There are no superheroes in the real world, but we're fascinated by them. From Batman to Spider-Man, superheroes are part of popular culture. What kind of jobs do you think present opportunities for being a hero? What are some good underlying motivations for being a hero? Think of some everyday examples that would allow ordinary people to take a stand and behave courageously.

5. Sometimes we want to do the right thing, but along the way we do the wrong thing in order to get to where we want to be. Mr. Incredible wants to stop a mugging, but when he is unable to, he throws his boss through some walls, injuring him severely. Every moral action we take has consequences: some good, some bad. What can you do to ensure that the moral choices you make are the best ones you can make? How can you avoid making bad moral decisions?

6. Mirage works for Syndrome, but later on in the movie she has a change of heart and decides to help Mr. Incredible. What brings about her change? Would you call her change a form of repentance? What is repentance, and what does it involve?

Cars

1. Cars come in many shapes, sizes, colors and speeds. If you could be a car, what kind of car would you be? A Porsche? A Buick? A Mazda? A big rig truck? Why?

2. Our culture places a lot of emphasis on cars and what kind of car someone drives. We sometimes see them as status symbols, especially if someone drives a luxury car or a fancy sports car. Yet every car is designed to get us from one place to another, and they all have the same basic functionality. Why do you think some people are so interested in cars and the kind of car they drive?

3. In *Cars*, Lightning McQueen finds himself on an unexpected adventure rather than the adventure he's used to (winning races). Have you ever found yourself on an unexpected adventure? What was it like? Did you learn anything of lasting value during your adventure?

4. Doc Hudson refers to his Piston Cup trophies as a bunch of empty cups. What does he mean by that? Lightning later says the same thing to Strip "The King" Weathers at the end of the race. What do you think Lightning has learned from Doc Hudson?

5. Mater is a simple, carefree tow truck who doesn't seem to care about appearances or status and who ends up being Lightning's best friend. How does their friendship grow?

6. When Lightning first tries to repair the road in Radiator Springs,

he does a terrible job because he is in a hurry to get it over with and get on his way to California. When Lightning takes his time and does the job right, the road turns out wonderfully. Why is it better to take the time to do something right rather than rushing things? How does this relate to our moral character?

Ratatouille

1. What are your favorite meals? What is it that you like about them? If you could go out to eat anywhere you wanted tonight, where would it be? What about the restaurant captures your interest?

2. Colette is a female chef struggling to succeed in a field dominated by men, and as a result has to work extra hard to prove herself. Is this fair? In an ideal world, would this be the case? What does Colette have to do in order to demonstrate that she has what it takes to get the job done? Have you ever worked in a setting in which your gender was in the minority? What did you learn from that experience?

3. How is cooking fine food comparable to composing music or painting a work of art? Why do we appreciate quality in the arts?

4. What do you think the Bible means when it says human beings are created in God's image? See Genesis 1:26-27. What does it *not* mean?

5. Think about positive and negative forms of ambition. What makes them different? Why is one form preferable while the other is not? Skim through chapter ten if you need to recall some of the ideas related to ambition that we covered.

6. Skinner, the owner of Gusteau's, is paranoid about Linguini's activities. He spies on him, tries to pull information out of him, calls in a lawyer to consult on things and begins to see every-

one as enemies. What kind of changes to Skinner's moral character would it take to turn him around as a person?

WALL-E

1. One hundred years ago, humans had not traveled to space, did not own personal computers, did not have televisions and did not use mobile phones or portable music players. What do you think the world will be like a hundred years from now? What is most plausible or implausible about the future as depicted in WALL-E (which is set in 2805)?

2. WALL-E is a robot, but he has a distinct personality. What human traits does he embody? What does he do that reminds you of yourself or your friends?

3. What does WALL-E suggest are the benefits of technology? The dangers?

4. What do you learn about human relationships from the interactions between WALL-E and EVE?

5. How might watching WALL-E change how you interact with personal technology and electronics?

6. Is it better to interact with a person electronically or face-to-face? What is gained by talking face-to-face? What is lost by interacting by text message, chat systems or email? Are some forms of communication better for some things than others?

Up

1. Have you ever met a dog like Dug? Dogs you have met don't talk, of course, but do they behave like Dug? Why do you think most dogs get excited and happy around people? Is there anything we can learn from their behavior?

2. How does Russell help Carl grow as a person? How does Carl help Russell?

3. We first meet Carl and Ellie when they are both children. They couldn't be more different: Ellie is outgoing and rambunctious, while Carl is shy and reserved. When two very different kinds of people like Carl and Ellie get married, how do their differences contribute positively to their relationship? How might their differences make their relationship more challenging?

4. Human beings seem hardwired to love and to be loved. How do you explain love in a world without God? In a world with God?

5. Adventurer Charles Muntz is obsessed with capturing the elusive Paradise Falls bird, dubbed "Kevin" by Russell. Why is Muntz so set on capturing Kevin? What does he want to prove? Has Muntz's obsession helped him grow positively or negatively in his moral character? How have his choices shaped his personality?

6. Carl eventually realizes that his life with Ellie was an adventure and that, even though she is gone, his life is still an adventure. God has in mind an adventure for each one of us that is unique, but too often we fail to see it because we are not looking at life the way God wants us to look at life. What can we do to be more attentive to the adventure God has called us to live?

NOTES

Chapter 1: Virtue & Wisdom

[1]Plato, *The Republic*, trans. R. E. Allen (New Haven, Conn.: Yale University Press, 2006), p. 146.

[2]John Milton, *Paradise Lost* (New York: Penguin Classics, 2003), p. 172.

Chapter 2: Hope & Imagination

[1]Cheryl Forbes, "Imagination," in *The Complete Book of Everyday Christianity*, ed. R. Paul Stevens and Robert J. Banks (Downers Grove, Ill.: InterVarsity Press, 1997), p. 516.

[2]Francis Schaeffer, *Art and the Bible*, IVP Classics ed. (Downers Grove, Ill.: InterVarsity Press, 2006), p. 91.

[3]John Weldon and James Bjornstad, *Playing with Fire* (Chicago: Moody Press, 1984), pp. 46-47.

[4]W. Harold Mare, Comments on 1 Corinthians 6:12-20, *Expositor's Bible Commentary*, vol. 10, ed. Frank Gaebelein (Grand Rapids: Zondervan, 2006), CD-ROM.

[5]D. A. Carson, Comments on Matthew 5:29-30, *Expositor's Bible Commentary*, vol. 8, ed. Frank Gaebelein (Grand Rapids: Zondervan, 1984), p. 151.

Chapter 4: Justice

[1]Karen Paik, *To Infinity and Beyond! The Story of Pixar Animation Studios* (San Francisco: Chronicle Books, 2007), p. 124.

Chapter 6: Humor

[1]*The Pixar Story*, DVD, directed by Leslie Iwerks (Santa Monica, Calif.: Leslie Iwerks Productions, 2007).

[2]Elton Trueblood, *The Humor of Christ* (San Francisco: Harper & Row, 1975), p. 15.

Chapter 9: Adventure
[1]J. R. R. Tolkien, *The Fellowship of the Ring* (New York: Ballantine Books), p. 110.
[2]Karen Paik, *To Infinity and Beyond! The Story of Pixar Animation Studios* (San Francisco: Chronicle Books, 2007), pp. 258-59.

Chapter 10: Ambition
[1]Andy Crouch, *Culture Making: Recovering Our Creative Calling* (Downers Grove, Ill.: InterVarsity Press, 2008), p. 23, italic in original.
[2]Os Guinness, *The Call: Finding and Fulfilling the Central Purpose of Your Life* (Nashville: Thomas Nelson, 1998), p. 73.

Chapter 11: Technology
[1]"Trivia for WALL-E," www.imdb.com/title/tt0910970/trivia.
[2]Jean Baudrillard, cited in Douglas Groothuis, *The Soul in Cyberspace* (Eugene, Ore.: Wipf & Stock, 1999), p. 78.

Chapter 12: Love
[1]Associated Press, "Dying Girl Gets Final Wish to See 'Up,'" CBS News website, www.cbsnews.com/stories/2009/06/19/national/main5098924.shtml.

FILMOGRAPHY

A Bug's Life. Directed by John Lasseter, codirected by Andrew Stanton. Emeryville, Calif.: Pixar Animation Studios, 1998.

Cars. Directed by John Lasseter, codirected by Joe Ranft. Emeryville, Calif.: Pixar Animation Studios, 2006.

Finding Nemo. Directed by Andrew Stanton, codirected by Lee Unkrich. Emeryville, Calif.: Pixar Animation Studios, 2003.

The Incredibles. Directed by Brad Bird. Emeryville, Calif.: Pixar Animation Studios, 2004.

Monsters, Inc. Directed by Pete Docter, codirected by David Silverman. Emeryville, Calif.: Pixar Animation Studios, 2001.

Pixar Short Film Collection, Volume 1. Emeryville, Calif.: Pixar Animation Studios, 2004.

The Pixar Story. Directed by Leslie Iwerks. Santa Monica, Calif.: Leslie Iwerks Productions, 2007.

Ratatouille. Directed by Brad Bird, codirected by Jan Pinkava. Burbank and Emeryville, Calif.: Walt Disney/Pixar Animation Studios, 2007.

Toy Story. Directed by John Lasseter. Emeryville, Calif.: Pixar Animation Studios, 1995.

Toy Story 2. Directed by John Lasseter, codirected by Ash Brannon and Lee Unkrich. Emeryville, Calif.: Pixar Animation Studios, 1999.

Up. Directed by Pete Docter, codirected by Bob Peterson. Burbank and Emeryville, Calif.: Walt Disney/Pixar Animation Studios, 2009.

WALL-E. Directed by Andrew Stanton. Burbank and Emeryville, Calif.: Walt Disney/Pixar Animation Studios, 2008.

ACKNOWLEDGMENTS

The *Wisdom of Pixar* is the product of many hours of research, writing, editing, thinking and, yes, watching Pixar films. This book also required the cooperation of a number of individuals, not the least of which was my family. My patient wife, Candace, once again accommodated my writing schedule with grace and understanding, and for this I offer my sincere and loving thanks. My four children also deserve a word of appreciation, although I must add that they enjoyed my work on *The Wisdom of Pixar* more than any other book project I've participated in thus far, often "suffering" with me as I watched Pixar films and key scenes repeatedly. Thanks, Anthony, Vincent, Dante and Marcus! Without each of you present, watching Pixar films would not have been nearly as fun. I must also offer special gratitude to the dedicated InterVarsity Press team. This is my third project with IVP and my second with editor Al Hsu, who, as always, provided excellent insights and suggestions along the way, for which I am grateful.

Pixar Index

The Pixar index contains a list of Pixar-related terms, films and fictional names. For the names of real-life individuals associated with Pixar, see the general index.

General Index